MW00965438

The Observant
LEADER

Warning Signals
That Can Cost You Your Job
and What to Do About Them

Wisdom from Successful Smaller
Not-for-Profit Organizations

Donald Ruhl

PETER E. RANDALL PUBLISHER
Portsmouth, New Hampshire
2021

ISBN: 978-1-937721-75-6
Library of Congress Control Number: 2021900801

Published by
Jetty House

an imprint of
Peter E. Randall Publisher
Portsmouth NH 03801
www.perpublisher.com

Book Design: Grace Peirce

This book is dedicated to my wife, Ellen Ruhl,
our daughters Beth and Heather,
and Richard E. Winslow III.

Contents

About the Author

Dr. Donald Ruhl is an organizational consultant specializing in not-for-profit organizations.

In addition to his teaching experience in two-year and four-year colleges and in universities, Dr. Ruhl has more than thirty years of experience working in leadership positions in not-for-profit organizations. These experiences, along with his chairmanship and membership on a variety of not-for-profit boards, has given him "on the firing line" expertise to write *The Observant Leader*.

Dr. Ruhl is Dean Emeritus of the College at Northern Essex Community College (Mass.) and the former President of Garrett Community College in Maryland. Dr. Ruhl served for fifteen years as the Executive Director and then President of the Greater Haverhill Chamber of Commerce in Massachusetts.

Dr. Ruhl is the co-author, with Dr. Howard Brown, of the pioneering book, *Breakthrough Management for Not-for-Profit Organizations: Beyond Survival in the 21st Century*. Dr Arthur Levine, former President of Teachers College, Columbia University, said of the book, "Brown and Ruhl have managed to produce an extraordinary volume that could become a new standard text both for individuals considering the not-for-profit field and those who are already professionals in the field."

Dr. Ruhl is also the author of two other books: *Survival Fundraising* and *The Happy Volunteer*.

Acknowledgments

This book is dedicated to my wife, Ellen Ruhl, my daughters Beth and Heather, and Richard E. Winslow III. My wife's continuing support and encouragement were critical to the successful completion of this book.

Special thanks are due to Barry Gorman for writing the foreword to this book. His insights are greatly appreciated!

The ideas presented and discussed in books are frequently the result of experiences which have taken place over an extended period of time. Mentors are of great importance in the continuing development and refinement of these ideas.

The author has been extremely fortunate to have had an outstanding group of mentors during his career. This group includes: Jack Armstrong, Ken Benne, Harold Bentley, Joseph Bevilacqua, Paul Bevilacqua, Charles Billups, Howard Brown, William Cavallaro, Roderick Condon II, John Dimitry, Eugene DuBois, Ferd Ensinger, Joseph Giampa, Gene Grillo, Malcolm Knowles, Arthur Levine, Stuart Marshall, William Nofsker, Barry Oshry, Gene Phillips, Robert Ramsey, John Ravekes, Lowell Trowbridge, Ed Veasey, and Robert Webber.

Special thanks go to Heather Kinsey for her superb work in providing technical support in the preparation of the manuscript.

The author appreciates the outstanding contributions of Peter E. Randall Publisher in making this book a reality. The team of Deidre Randall, Grace Peirce, and Zak Johnson has been highly supportive throughout this project.

Foreword

At first glance one might well wonder why a former soccer coach is penning a foreword for a not-for-profit book "The Observant Leader." To be completely frank, if anyone had even suggested I knew anything about not-for-profit groups when I embarked on a teaching and coaching pathway in Belfast, Northern Ireland many years ago, those who knew me then, would collapse in fits of laughter.

Of course, that was long before I was introduced to Dr. Don Ruhl and got to know him. Often throughout one's career, we reflect on such introductions and question why this acquaintance didn't occur earlier in one's own professional development and what relevance it actually has with one's chosen profession. It was after spending hours in casual discussion with Don Ruhl about his career in education and business that similarities between his not-for-profit work and my chosen coaching profession started to become evident.

Dealing in depth with the many facets of support systems that surround the functioning of Olympic sports, one only truly appreciates the connection with volunteer organizations when they meet someone as knowledgeable and experienced as Don Ruhl.

In breaking down his masterful insights into leadership, only then do you start to garner the importance of the "transfer of learning" factor from one work endeavor to another. Whereas leaders in all industries depend on trusted hired full-time employees, many don't realize the full extent to which there is an army of volunteers toiling in the trenches. It is the guidance of the organization's overall associated members that Dr. Ruhl so comprehensively addresses in "The Observant Leader" that ensures that the association's foundation and leadership remain on solid ground.

It was the leadership similarities to coaching that Dr. Ruhl's research unearthed that I found fascinating when I first read his earlier book "The Happy Volunteer." "The Observant Leader" delves more deeply into the leadership role and its impact on the broader aspects of society. As Dr. Ruhl rightly points out, many not-for-profit organizations support the development of good physical and mental health, as well as the pursuit of excellence and the attributes of good citizenship. It is, therefore, not a stretch to substitute the term leader/coach/sport when discussing these qualities.

In the modern era, longevity among leaders, in all fields, is as rare as finding dinosaur bones in your backyard. The keys to a successful long-time career are clearly outlined in "The Observant Leader" which provides priceless nuggets of wisdom to individuals in leadership positions in organizations of all sizes.

For any leader to have a long-term meaningful impact, time and continuity are paramount. However due to limited financial resources, costly ever-changing technology, lack of experience in trained adaptive and flexible management skills, time is not a commodity often afforded to today's leaders in modern times where instant success is expected. As in leading a smaller not-for-profit organization, coaching an Olympic sport requires a depth of expertise and understanding of what internal and external influences are affecting leadership decisions. Regardless of their role, the difficulties and complexities facing a leader's ability to function have multiplied, one hundred-fold on all fronts, as via multimedia anyone can scrutinize every decision in real time.

One of the many problems that occur with multimedia browsing is that those using it merely gloss over the "highlight reels" and fail to grasp a true appreciation of what is involved when passing judgement on a leader's decision-making process. Typically, these people have never been personally involved in leadership and management positions of any real meaning.

Worse still are those who have only theoretical backgrounds and have never personally faced the pressure of immediate decisions that affect the livelihood of their employees. They lack what Dr. Ruhl terms the "emotional intelligence" true leaders, like coaches, possess having been forced to make cutting edge decisions in the heat of competition. All this while under pressure to discover opportunities in the face of adversity, and having enough courage to overcome the "fear of failure" is a true hallmark of battle-hardened leaders. Such leaders have maintained high levels of self-confidence, self-esteem and unwavering belief embedded in a strong commitment to helping fulfill the mission of the organization, while at the same time, remaining humble and recognizing the contributions of their staff and volunteers. This is where intelligent savvy leaders ensure that they have a supportive collection of influential knowledge-able people forming an inner core who are also fully committed to the organization/team/sport's long-term success.

Furthermore, as Don Ruhl points out, an obser-vant leader and his trusted staff must be vigilant of potentially erosive warning signals that may damage an organization's functioning. Again, the parallels with the instability within any coaching ranks are plainly obvious if a coach/leader doesn't surround him/herself with trusted knowledgeable assistants and volunteers that complement his/her skill set. Whereas Dr. Ruhl is concerned about short-term lead-ership turnover in not-for-profit organizations, many of us in the coaching world are apprehensive about the managerial hiring and firing "merry-go-round" that has become a feature in all sports today.

As surely as the earth rotates, the world is ever changing and perceptive leaders should be proac-tively vigilant in identifying both positive and nega-tive internal and external alarms.

Therefore, assessing an organization's strengths and weaknesses while being fully aware of one's own strengths and shortcomings contributes to a strong foundation from which to determine the importance of the numerous influential intangibles. Successful coaches like CEOs learn how to gather a staff that is supportive yet willing to challenge the establishment to strive for greater achievements. It is with this in mind that Don Ruhl strongly cautions leaders to be cognizant of what he terms "backstabbers."

Regretfully, backstabbers may come in two invisible forms. Both question any long-term leader's management style which they may see as "Old School" and feel there is an abrupt need for immediate "changing of the guard." The "deliberate-backstabber" is someone who knowingly undermines the establishment in the name of revolution, fresh ideas and self-promotion. He sees himself as irreplaceable to the organization and an heir/heiress apparent. The "unwitting or reluctant backstabber" is someone who pushes for reforms without thinking through long term goals and the impact on the organization's/program's long serving members. Unfortunately, both types of backstabbers lack experience and depth of knowledge to comprehend the bigger picture and fail to realize the time and effort that went into forging multiple connections to build lasting trusted networks.

Dr. Ruhl knows only too well how mobilizing community resources and expanding capacity through "happy engaged volunteers" enhances an organization's general profile, to attract more connected volunteers, qualified participants, and important program funding. Whereas innovation and creativity are prerequisites, loyalty and commitment to the program mission/goals and leadership are essential if a team/ sport/business is to function efficiently year after year. The fear is that too much change often blurs mission lines and causes a shift away from an organization's purpose. To this end, "The Observant Leader" can differentiate between the people wanting to paint the wheel a different color and present it as something new and those intelligent individuals who improve the wheel's overall efficiency and attractiveness.

In the short and the long term, smaller not-for-profits, such as sports organizations, deal with essential fundamental leadership management issues in order to survive and prosper. Smaller not-for-profits can and do provide a role model for many other organizations/associations/teams because they have to pay careful attention to day-to-day, month-to-month and year-to-year essentials in order to last and thrive.

— *Barry Gorman, Penn State head soccer coach (1987 to 2009) and past president of the National Soccer Coaches Association of America (United Soccer Coaches)*.*

*Barry Gorman's coaching career is nothing short of legendary, having coached Penn State's teams to 254 victories in twenty-two seasons, including twelve NCAA tournament appearances and three post-season Big Ten Tournament championships. His personal honors include three NSCAA Regional Coach of the Year awards.

Introduction

Background: The "Observant Leader"

A major problem today in many smaller not-for-profit organizations is the short length of time that their leaders remain in their positions. We are living in an age of "transitory leadership." This is true for many reasons. It may be a question of leadership style, lack of commitment, financial instability, lack of loyalty, changes in the environment, or a variety of other reasons. In many cases, the leader may be asked to resign.

The result of such short-term leadership is that the contributions of the leader are frequently of little consequence. Positive leadership impact on an organization requires time.

Organizational excellence requires excellent ongoing leadership. In order to sustain leadership and organizational excellence, there has to be some continuity and consistency.

One of the important purposes of this book is to help leaders of smaller not-for-profits keep their jobs, thereby increasing their contributions and legacy as leaders. In order to do this, they need to be keen observers of the internal and external environments in which they operate.

"Observant Leaders" need to be aware of and act on a variety of warning signals in the environments in which they operate which represent present or future problems. This book discusses warning signals that can alert you, as the leader, of the need to take action before a problem or potential problem becomes more acute. Specific action strategies are suggested to deal with these warning signals. The warning signals discussed in this book have been included because of their importance and the frequency with which they occur.

Being proactive is one of the key ingredients in successful leadership in smaller not-for-profit organizations. These organizations are more vulnerable in many ways because they lack resources in key management areas as well as other areas. Because of this, they need to act more quickly to remedy present and potential problems. In order to do this, as mentioned previously, they must be keen observers of the environments in which they operate. In addition, they need to have insight into their own values, beliefs, and competencies as they impact the ways in which they perceive and act on these environmental situations.

The central focus of the "Observant Leader" is that identifying and acting on warning signals of present and potential problem areas is critical for personal and organizational survival and prosperity in smaller not-for-profits. Some of these warning signals involve specific individuals, some involve groups, and others may involve the organization as a whole.

In smaller not-for-profits, each individual must perform well if the organization is to succeed. These organizations do not have the resources to cover up for non-performers. Individuals must pull their own weight. The "Observant Leader" needs to be aware of the strengths and weaknesses of each employee. Having this knowledge will enable the leader to work with employees to build on their strengths and minimize their weaknesses. The importance of being aware of group and broad-based organizational warning signals is also discussed in this book.

The "Observant Leader" discusses ways in which warning signals and the problems connected with them can be converted into opportunities for positive action which will improve the health and contributions of a smaller not-for-profit organization. At a personal level, converting problem areas into success stories is a great way for not-for-profit leaders to demonstrate their value to their organizations.

The ability to identify areas of organizational difficulty and create out of them areas of excellence can be one of the most satisfying aspects of leadership. A central characteristic of successful not-for-profit organizations is their capacity to creatively discover and act on opportunities to improve their performance as they work to serve their constituents.

Organization of the Book

The "Observant Leader" consists of a foreword, six chapters, and a concluding section:

- Chapter 1: Warning Signals: Problems with the Leader
- Chapter 2: Warning Signals: Problems with the Mission
- Chapter 3: Warning Signals: Problems with the Board
- Chapter 4: Warning Signals: Problems within the Organization
- Chapter 5: Warning Signals: Problems outside the Organization
- Chapter 6: Wisdom from the "Observant Leader"

Chapter 1 deals with warning signals concerning the personal characteristics of leaders that can get them into trouble.

Chapter 2 explains the central importance of the mission and warning signals concerning it. It deals with warning signals concerning the mission itself, commitment to the mission, and communicating about the mission.

Chapter 3 discusses warning signals regarding the Boards of smaller not-for-profit organizations. Among the warning signals are those dealing with roles and responsibilities, commitment to the mission, under-standing the special characteristics of a not-for-profit organization, the Board selection process, and the Board Chair-Leader relationship.

Chapter 4 deals with warning signals within the organization that represent problems of organizational health. Warning signals regarding the "tone" of the organization are discussed in some detail. These include the level of innovation, creativity, morale, complexity, participation, trust, loyalty, optimism, energy, fun, and enthusiasm in an organization which can be important indicators of present or potential problems. Various warning signals regarding a breakdown in communication processes are also highlighted.

Chapter 5 focuses on warning signals in the environments outside of the organization. Warning signals concerning the media, changes in the economic, political and social environments, and the personal support system of the leader are among the issues which are discussed.

Chapter 6 serves as a way to re-emphasize some key points presented earlier in the book as well as to introduce some new materials that the author believes to be of significant importance to the leadership practitioner in smaller not-for-profit organizations. The ideas presented in this chapter deal with leadership mindset and behavior, Board behavior, focusing on and sustaining the mission, financial well-being, awareness of and communication with the internal and external environments of the organization, the identification of "back stabbers", and suggestions for keeping your job.

Who Should Read this Book?

You should read this book if:

- You are interested in spotting warning signals that threaten your success as a leader.
- You are interested in acting to deal with present and potential problems before they cost you your job.
- You are interested in keeping your job long enough to have a positive impact on the organization where you are currently working.
- You are interested in knowing what is really going on in your organization.
- You are interested in being a more effective and successful leader.
- You want your present job to be more interesting, meaningful, and rewarding.
- You are a Board member of a not-for-profit organization.
- You are interested in the success of not-for-profit organizations.

How is this Book Different?

How is this book different from the typical book about leadership? This book is based upon the author's observations and experiences in the field. It is not based upon the ideas of people who have never been personally involved in leadership and management positions.

In addition to his teaching experience in two year and four year colleges and in universities, the author has more than thirty years of experience working as a leader in not-for-profit organizations. The warning signals discussed in this book are based upon his personal experiences and observations during this period of time. Dr. Ruhl believes that one has to experience and observe the emotional as well as the intellectual challenges faced by leaders in order to really understand what is required to be a successful leader. One has to be a practitioner as well as a theoretician in order to understand the action strategies that are required.

Most books on leadership and management discuss leadership in terms of desired characteristics and behaviors. This book is different because it deals with the identification of warning signals concerning specific situations that require action if the leader and the organization are to be successful. This book is also different because it focuses on warning signals in smaller not-for-profit organizations which concern issues of critical importance in these complex institutions.

The great majority of smaller not-for-profit organizations have relatively few full-time employees. They frequently have a number of part-time employees and are often dependent as well on a group of volunteers. These organizations are often involved in a struggle for survival because of their limited human and financial resources and require excellent leadership if they are to be successful. Their leaders must be keen observers of the internal and external environments in which they work. They must be aware of the warning signals which indicate threats to their personal and organizational success. They need to be able to act quickly if they are to successfully meet the challenges facing them. They do not have the staying power to deal with these threats on a long-term basis. It is easy for leaders in smaller not-for-profit organizations to miss important warning signals because they are caught up in a flurry of activities dealing with inadequate resources, dependence upon public and private sector organizations, a broad range of constituencies, and the management of volunteers along with a variety of other issues.

And Finally...

The author wrote this book in order to help people in leadership positions in smaller not-for-profit organizations identify and act on warning signals that threaten their personal success and the success of their organizations. It is his belief that not-for-profit organizations are a critically important part of the fabric of American society. Many of these not-for-profit organizations have a small staff and have limited resources with which to operate. In order to be successful they have to have consistent ongoing first rate leadership.

The author of this book is concerned about the turnover rate of leaders in smaller not-for-profit organizations. By identifying and acting on present and potential warning signals, it is his hope that the longevity of these leaders in their positions, as well as their contributions to their organizations and the clients they serve can be increased. To have impact as a leader requires time and continuity.

It is also the author's hope that as a result of this book there will be a better understanding of the difficulty and complexity of the leadership function in smaller not-for-profit organizations.

Leading a smaller not-for-profit organization with its limited human, technical, and financial resources requires an understanding of what is really happening in the internal and external environments in which the leadership is taking place. It requires an "Observant Leader."

It is the hope of the author that Board members of smaller not-for-profit organizations who read this book will gain a further appreciation of leadership in these organizations. Boards are a key ingredient in the success or failure of leaders in smaller not-for-profit organizations. A supportive Board can make a great difference in the ability of a leader to lead with confidence and excellence.

CHAPTER 1

Problems with the Leader

"A warning signal in receiving communication feedback is a lack of diversity in the people providing it."

Problems with the Leader

Warning Signal
No. 1
Is Not Fully Committed to Achieving the Mission

The purpose of the not-for-profit organization is to achieve its mission. Its purpose is not to make a profit. The "Observant Leader" has to keep this fact clearly in mind. The leader not only has to keep the mission in mind at all times, but needs to have an overwhelming commitment to working toward its successful accomplishment through a variety of activities that support it.

In smaller not-for-profit organizations with their limited human, financial, and technical resources, there is the danger that the mission can be forgotten in the press of immediate day-to-day activities. The mission can be sidetracked for non-mission-oriented activities which are of minor importance. Specific problems which involve the mission will be discussed at some length in chapter 2: "Problems with the Mission."

The "Observant Leader" must not only be fully committed to successfully accomplishing the mission but also to making it understandable and relevant to all the members of the organization. "Observant Leaders" must communicate through action, their unswerving commitment to the mission. This message must be strong and clear. If you, as the "Observant Leader," examine your personal commitment to the mission and find it wanting, this is a warning signal to you. You need to discover what problems are keeping you from an all-out commitment. Without such a commitment, you, as the leader, will find it difficult, if not impossible, to lead with vision, energy, and enthusiasm. It is of critical importance to your personal success and the success of the organization that you examine on a continuing basis the level of commitment that you have to the work you are doing. It is easy for your commitment to falter without fully realizing it. If, after a strong effort on your part, you can't re-energize your commitment to the mission of your organization, it may be time for you to move on to other challenges. Taking short periods of time away from the job can sometimes be of real value if this is a possibility for you.

A friend of the author who has served in a leadership role in a number of not-for-profit organizations shared this quotation, "I find that I can't do twelve months work in twelve months but that I can do twelve months work in eleven months."

Successful leadership in smaller not-for-profit organizations requires a strong commitment to mission. It is important that you, as the "Observant Leader," keep checking your level of commitment and work to keep it at a high level if you wish to be such a successful leader.

Warning Signal
No. 2
Lack of Self-Esteem and Self-Confidence

If you, as a leader of a smaller not-for-profit orga-nization, are lacking in self-esteem and self-confi-dence, you will need to do something about it if you are going to be successful. It is the author's view that it is highly unlikely that an individual with low self-es-teem and self-confidence will be able to provide the vision, confidence, and energy to deal with the rigors of successfully leading a smaller not-for-profit orga-nization. Good self-esteem and self-confidence are prerequisites for dynamic proactive leadership.

A good place to start in working to improve your self-esteem and self-confidence is the work of Nathaniel Branden. The author has found Branden's books to be useful in thinking about the importance of good self-esteem to the practitioner in the field. Branden believes that self-efficacy and self-respect are indispensable components of self-esteem. Self-efficacy means that you feel capable of dealing with life's chal-lenges and self-respect that you believe yourself to be a worthy human being.

The author believes that most people are capable of achieving a great deal and that they are frequently using only a small part of their capabilities. The author also believes that it is a common thing for people to undervalue their capabilities. This tendency to undervalue one's own abilities and believe that other people are more competent than they may actually be can be a major barrier to taking important action as a leader. It is important that you have a level of self-esteem and self-confidence that enables you to recognize your personal strengths, develop them further, and use them productively to achieve personal and organizational goals. Having the courage to develop your personal strengths and use them to benefit your organization and the broader society is at the heart of being a great leader.

Realizing the importance of good self-esteem and self-confidence, leaders will also want to help to develop these attributes in other members of the organization. This is especially important in smaller not-for-profit organizations where each member of the organization is required to function at a high level because of the limited human resources which are available. The "Observant Leader" should be concerned, on a continuing basis, with discovering the strengths of the members of the organization and helping them to further develop and utilize these strengths.

The leader who does not value himself or herself will find it difficult to value the other members of the organization. Not-for-profit organizations are in the self-esteem building "business." The presence of low self-esteem and low self-confidence in an organization is a significant warning signal to the "Observant Leader" that immediate action steps must be taken to create a culture of optimism and a belief in the organization's ability at both the personal and organizational level to achieve desired outcomes. Successes must be widely communicated and celebrated to reinforce the fact that the individuals involved have the capacity and the willingness to achieve great things. The goal is to build a sustainable culture with self-esteem and self-confidence as key building blocks.

Warning Signal
No. 3
Allowing Unfounded Fears to Undermine Your Success

What fears do you, in a leadership role in a smaller not-for-profit organization, have that can undermine your self-confidence and your success? Are these fears real or imagined? The "Observant Leader" recommends that you be proactive in analyzing the validity of your fears. A thoughtful analysis will show that in many cases, these fears are unfounded. If, however, your analysis shows that a fear is based on legitimate concerns, you need to be proactive in carefully weighing the advantages and disadvantages of your plan before taking action.

The "Observant Leader" knows that while fears can be immobilizing, they can also be of value in encouraging an intelligent analysis in the decision-making process. Be careful not to let fears of imaginary, non-existent obstacles deter you, as the "Observant Leader," from identifying and being proactive regarding the opportunities that must be acted upon if your organization is to be innovative, unique, and a leader in your areas of service. At the same time, it is important that the leader carefully consider fears that are based on legitimate concerns that may pose real threats to his or her success and the success of the organization.

Fears that are Sometimes Part of the Leadership Experience:

- Losing your job if things don't work out well.
- Not having the personal competencies to lead a particular project.
- Not having the necessary technical competencies.
- Not getting the support of your people.
- Your ideas will be perceived as too radical by the board.
- Your network of friends will be unhappy with you.
- Key people in your organization will be offended by your actions.
- The future of your organization will be endangered if the effort at hand is unsuccessful.
- This is a departure from what your organization has done in the past.
- You don't have the necessary human resources.
- You don't have the necessary financial resources.
- You don't have the required technical resources.
- The risk is too great.
- You don't have all the information required to make an informed decision.

Overcoming fear is an important part of good leadership. In fact, it is an essential part of the leadership process. It takes courage to successfully lead a smaller not-for-profit organization. The challenges are many, but, by the same token, the personal satisfaction can be great. It is these smaller not-for-profit organizations that play a critically important role in helping to build a society that values human growth and development.

A majority of not-for-profit organizations are smaller in their number of employees, but their combined efforts can have a profound positive impact on the quality of life in the local communities they serve and in the broader society.

Fear can be a major obstacle in inhibiting the actions that are required to maximize the positive impact of smaller not-for-profit organizations. The leaders and boards of these organizations have to exhibit courage in the face of fear and uncertainty. They have to have the courage to master fear and move forward in experimenting with and implementing new and better ways of serving their various constituencies. The boards of these organizations have a critical role to play in supporting courageous actions on the part of their leaders. Boards have to encourage and support the efforts of their leaders to move out of their comfort zones in creating new and different approaches to meet the needs of the publics they serve. Smaller not-for-profit organizations, in their role as creative and innovative change agents in their communities, should be in the forefront in leading the charge to find and implement new and better ways to improve the human condition in their areas of service. This requires the courage to be different and better. The "Observant Leader," with the support of his or her board, is a key figure in the process of societal transformation.

Warning Signal
No. 4
Lack of Trust and Respect in the Leader/ Board-Chair Relationship

The leader of a not-for-profit organization is responsible for the operational side of the organization. The board of directors has fiscal responsibility for the organization as well as the responsibility for approving its policies. The board also has the responsibility for hiring, supervising, and if necessary, terminating the service of the leader. The board is led by a chairman. The board chair and the members of the board are, in most cases, volunteers who are not financially compensated for their services. We have here the interesting situation of a paid leader who is responsible to a board of unpaid volunteers.

The leader-board chair relationship is a critical component in the functioning of a smaller not-for-profit organization. If this relationship is not one of mutual respect and trust the leader is in serious trouble. This is true because the board chair is the key link in the leader-board relationship.

The leader and the board chair have to work as a dynamic team that drives and sustains the vision and mission of the organization. They have to be on the same page! The board chair has to be a supporter and advocate of the initiatives of the leader if the leader is to be successful. It is essential that the board chair work diligently with the board to create a spirit of cooperation and support with the leader and the leadership team.

It is extremely important that the leader pay a great deal of attention to the relationship with the board chair. Building this relationship should be a number one priority. The leader and the board chair should have both a good professional and personal relationship. The personal as well as the professional relationship between them is important. They must trust and respect each other.

As the leader of a smaller not-for-profit organization you should insist on having input into the selection of the board chair. You should also have input into the selection of individual board members. Such involvement can frequently avoid adversarial relationships down the road.

Some characteristics of a desirable board chair are included in chapter 6: "Wisdom from the 'Observant Leader'" in a "Wish List Concerning a Board Chair."

In the observations of the author, as a practitioner in the field, the success of leaders in smaller not-for-profit organizations has been closely related to the quality of the leader/board-chair relationship. If you want to keep your job as the leader, pay a great deal of attention to this relationship.

The leader/board-chair relationship is especially important in smaller not-for-profit organizations because of its visibility to the people who work in these organizations. A good working relationship between the leader and the board chair is readily noticed in smaller, less-formal, less-structured organizations.

Seeing a relationship of good feeling and mutual trust along with a strong commitment to the goals of the organization gives a sense of confidence to the people who work for the organization. This good feeling, mutual trust, and commitment to the mission in the leader/board-chair relationship supports a similar feeling in the full board and is also a strong signal to the organization's supporters and constituents that the leadership and the board have their act together.

Warning Signal
No. 5
Getting Too Far Ahead of the Board

Boards of directors of smaller not-for-profit organizations are frequently more conservative than their leaders. As the leader of a not-for-profit organization, you should be aware of this situation.

Possible reasons for boards being more conservative than their leaders might include their fiscal responsibility for the institution, their unwillingness to take risks for a mission to which they are not fully committed, or their need to take a middle course in order to get their members with differing points of view to come to an agreement.

Disagreements between leaders and their boards of directors may involve philosophy, financial expenditures, customers to be served, the institutional service area, best ways to achieve the mission, the required level of financial reserves, construction of new facilities, personnel policies, or a number of other issues.

The relationship between the leader and the board chair is of critical importance in working out the differences that are involved. The board chair not only has to be fully informed about planned initiatives of the leader and the leadership team, but needs to be fully committed to these initiatives if they are to be successfully implemented. The board chair has to be a champion for the proposed ventures with the membership of the board. This is easier with a small board where the chair can meet personally with each board member to discuss the issues at hand. With larger boards, the chair will need to work closely with the executive committee in communication efforts with the full board. Laying the groundwork for planned initiatives is extremely important.

A failure to close the gap between the positions and actions of the leader and the board may result in the leader losing his or her job. "Observant Leaders" make it a point to examine the alignment of their thinking, attitudes, and actions with the thinking, attitudes, and actions of the board on a continuing basis in order to identify and realign significant discrepancies.

Warning Signal
No. 6
Not Having Enough True Allies/Friends in Key Positions Inside and Outside the Organization

Here we are talking about allies/friends you, as the leader, can trust to support you and your initiatives when the going gets tough. Unfortunately, it is frequently the case that "loyal" supporters disappear when difficult times occur. The applause is loud when the organization is doing well, but there is a mass exodus when difficulties occur.

It is important that the "Observant Leader" be aware, to the extent possible, of "false friends." These "false friends" tend to be interested primarily in their own advancement in the organization. They appear to be team players, but, in reality, care only about their personal success. At their very worst, they are back stabbers who feign friendship and loyalty only to further their own personal goals.

In building a network of true allies/friends with whom you, as the leader, have a relationship of mutual trust there are a number of areas that should be of special concern. The relationship with the board chair is, of course, of critical importance. The board chair has to be a true ally if you are to succeed in your job as the leader of a not-for-profit organization. It is also important that the leader develop a personal relationship with as many members of the board as possible. This ability to develop a relationship with each board member is aided when the board is smaller in size. The author of this book argues for the desirability of a smaller board in the section of the book dealing with boards. If the board is a large one it is extremely important that the leader develop a relationship of trust with the members of the executive committee. Board members have to be allies not antagonists if the leader is to be successful.

Another key relationship is with the chief financial officer whose honesty, competence, and loyalty are essential in keeping your financial house in order. It is also important that there be a high level of mutual trust with the leaders of the informal power structure that exists in your not-for-profit organization. These informal leaders, who do not appear on the formal organization chart, can be some of your most important allies/friends in difficult times. They are able to influence their fellow employees in the organization because they have been identified by these employees as people whose advice and counsel they value. In addition, it is important for the leader to build a strong sense of mutual trust with the members of the administrative management team. The leader needs to stress the point through action that the members of the management team can best advance their own personal goals by being team players and supporting each other and the leader as they pursue the organizational mission.

It is also important for the leader to have allies/friends outside of the organization. Allies in the community at large, including the political, business, and educational communities, are essential for the leader personally and for the organization as a whole if the not-for-profit organization is to successfully pursue its goals. These community allies can be extremely useful in getting their friends and associates to become advocates for your not-for-profit organization. They can also be extremely important in helping to work through problem areas with community members who have an antagonistic relationship with you and your organization. These community allies can sometimes achieve positive outcomes that you, as a leader, might not be able to achieve on your own.

In smaller not-for-profit organizations with their limited human, financial, and technical resources it is essential that people pull together if they are to be successful. Smaller not-for-profits are vulnerable in many ways. The leader and the organization need as many allies and friends as possible. The leader needs to lead the way to build a network of allies and friends who will continue to be supportive of the leadership, the organization, and the mission in difficult times.

Warning Signal
No. 7
Failing to See and Act on Opportunities

The ability to see and act on opportunities is of critical importance in smaller not-for-profit organizations. This is because smaller not-for-profits are, in many cases, specializing in specific niches in the human improvement field. They need to be focused on what they do and they have to be creative and innovative in doing it. They are not built for the high-volume provision of services and goods. They need to keep moving on to discover new ways to better serve their clients with the limited resources at their disposal. They may also discover ways to partner with other not-for-profits with similar goals while retaining their unique identity and contributions.

A significant advantage that smaller not-for-profit organizations have going for them is the fact that they are usually much less bureaucratic in nature. They are generally able to move with greater agility and speed to meet emerging needs in their fields of human improvement work.

The leader must be able to identify these emerging opportunities and mobilize the resources to take advantage of them. It is a warning signal to the leader if new opportunities are not being found for organizational involvement. It is important to ask why new opportunities are not being discovered. Is it a question of not knowing what business the not-for-profit organization is really in; of defining it too narrowly? Is it a question of not fully understanding the mission? Is it a question of not knowing how to make the organization different and better? Is it a fear of trying new things? Is it a lack of institutional self-confidence and expertise? Is it the result of inadequate feedback from the external environments in which the organization operates?

Whatever it is, it is important that the "Observant Leader" initiate action to deal with the specific problems that have been identified.

A major job of the "Observant Leader" is to discover new opportunities for the organization to be of service and have a real impact for the better in the organization's service area. The ability to spot and capitalize on new opportunities, both for the leader personally and for the organization, is an important ingredient for success.

With regard to personal leadership success, the author of this book remembers a conversation he had with a highly successful executive about his career. The executive stressed the importance of recognizing and taking advantage of opportunities. He emphasized that a major reason for his success was the fact that he had attempted and been successful doing things in his career that other people believed were not permitted by the rules and regulations of the organization. As a result of successfully doing what others felt was not possible, he had been promoted to increasingly responsible positions while they had failed to advance their careers.

Warning Signal
No. 8
Lack of Clear Short-Term Priorities and Goals

A warning signal for the "Observant Leader" is the failure to have clear, mission-oriented, short-term priorities and goals. A major reason that clear, motivating, mission-oriented, short-term goals are so important is that they are an effective way to keep leaders from spending a great deal of time on activities that have little or nothing to do with the missions of their organizations.

The leaders of smaller not-for-profits are, in many cases, under considerable pressure to deal with a large number of routine decisions which should be handled by other people in the organization. Rather than dealing with the few important decisions that would really make a difference in moving their organization ahead, they get bogged down with unimportant matters.

Keeping short-term priorities and goals clearly in mind forces the "Observant Leader" to develop strategies to take care of as much of the routine decision-making as possible in other ways. Developing carefully thought-through policies, procedures, and systems can be an important part of the process.

"Observant Leaders" have to learn to deal with the regular occurrence of "emergency decisions." To the person approaching the leader for a decision, that decision is an emergency. The person requesting the decision wants an immediate response because of the sense of urgency. The reality may be that the decision which is requested is unimportant and does not require immediate attention. As noted previously, "Observant Leaders" need, to the extent possible, to learn how to spend their time on the few things that really make a difference for the success of the organization. In his book, *Community Colleges: A President's View*, Thomas O'Connell makes the point that some of the worst leaders deal brilliantly with things as they come through the door. The problem is that they may have little or nothing to do with priorities. Peter Drucker in his writings stresses the importance of the leader focusing on the few things that really make a difference for the organization.

It must be stressed that the short-term priorities and goals that we are talking about should be directly related to the long-term priorities necessary to successfully achieve the mission of the organization. Successfully achieving the short-term goals provides the leader and the not-for-profit organization with benchmarks of success that build a sense of confidence and are motivating in keeping the organization on the move. Successfully achieving these short-term goals is important in providing positive motivating feedback. It is important that successes in achieving short-term goals be recognized and celebrated on a continuing basis.

Warning Signal
No. 9
Lack of Accurate and Balanced Feedback

"Observant Leaders" need to receive accurate and balanced communication feedback if they are to function effectively on a personal and organizational level. It is critically important that they receive feedback that is accurate and balanced if they are to make the best possible decisions. They need to know what is really going on in the internal and external environments in which they operate.

There is a great deal of incorrect or partially correct information that occurs within and outside of an organization. Believing and acting on erroneous information can result in decisions that may have devastating consequences for smaller not-for-profit organizations which have a very small margin for error because of their limited resources. They do not have the ability to withstand setbacks that larger organizations could overcome.

Inaccurate communication feedback comes in many forms. A common example is the expression "they say": "they say morale is low," "they say we are in financial trouble," "they say there will be layoffs." The "Observant Leader" asks the question—who says and attempts to discover the real story behind the "they say" comments.

Another example of inaccurate or partially correct feedback which can be a big problem involves people reporting directly to the leader. Frequently, the person doing the reporting gives the leader only good news. Reporting bad news is rarely a comfortable process. The practice of reporting only good news to the boss can result in very serious problems for the leader who suddenly discovers that there is a crisis situation of which he or she was completely unaware.

It is important that leaders develop information systems that provide reliable, accurate information on a consistent ongoing basis. This information informs the "Observant Leader" about what is happening in both the internal and external environments with which the organization interfaces. These systems should include feedback from individuals, small groups, and the organization as a whole.

Developing and sustaining these feedback relationships should usually be easier to do in smaller less formal, less structured, less rigid organizations. This is an advantage that you should capitalize on as the leader of such an organization. With regard to accessing information about what is happening in the external environment, your smaller not-for-profit organization may find it useful to build relationships with other organizations and information gathering entities to augment your organization's own information gathering capacity.

It is important in communication feedback that an environment is created that encourages honest, open, informed interaction. For this to happen, there must be a sense of trust that the feedback will not result in penalizing the people providing it, but rather that their observations will be appreciated and perceived as being of value to the organization.

A warning signal in receiving communication feedback is a lack of diversity in the people providing it. It is a warning signal to the "Observant Leader" if feedback is coming from only one individual or one group. Balance is extremely important in the sources from which communication feedback is received. Diversity of input is necessary in order to provide the framework that supports good decision making on the part of the leaders of smaller not-for-profits who, as mentioned previously, frequently have little room for error.

Warning Signal
No. 10
Speaking More Than You Listen

In order to determine whether the information which is being received is accurate and balanced, the "Observant Leader" needs to develop good listening skills. Among the major barriers to being a really good listener is the common belief that leaders need to do most of the talking and the fact that many people are carefully trained to be experts in determining what is wrong with something rather than trying to understand the relevance and significance of the information that is being presented.

With regard to the first of the significant barriers to good listening, the belief that leaders need to do most of the talking, such behavior frequently results in a failure to receive information that is essential to good decision making on the part of the leader. The leader who insists on dominating the communication process will frequently interrupt communication and shut off or discourage important feedback. This tendency on the part of the leader to interject his or her "wisdom" can be very discouraging to people trying their best to provide important feedback.

This is especially true of people providing the feedback who were not eager to provide it in the first place. The "Observant Leader" understands that good leadership involves the self-discipline to overcome the tendency to interrupt the communication flow to meet one's ego needs.

With regard to the second major barrier to good listening: being carefully trained to be an "expert in criticism," the major difficulty is that the leader isn't really listening to understand the information being presented in a comprehensive and insightful manner. Premature judgment about what is being communicated undermines the ability of the leader to creatively listen to and understand what is being communicated.

It is a warning signal if you, as a leader, find that you are talking far too much on a regular basis as well as being an "expert in criticism." Make every effort to listen more and to withhold judgment until you have listened to a communication in its entirety.

Warning Signal
No. 11
Having an Inadequate Understanding of Finance

The fact that achieving the mission is the most important purpose of the not-for-profit organization doesn't mean that the financial well-being of the organization isn't important. A not-for-profit organization that is in poor financial condition suffers in many ways. The impact of financial difficulties on the overall organization is discussed in detail in chapter 6: "Wisdom from the 'Observant Leader.'" The productivity and morale of the organization can be severely affected and its future existence threatened. Poor financial functioning can completely undermine the organization's mission and the job of the leader can be placed in great jeopardy. In the experience of the author of this book, financial difficulties are probably the most frequent reason for the firing or the resignation of leaders of smaller not-for-profit organizations. The "Observant Leader" must be aware of the financial vulnerability of smaller not-for-profits and the urgent need to pay attention to the warning signals that threaten their survival. Among these warning signals are declining enrollments, declining membership, declining contributions, a declining economy, self-serving board members with expensive agendas, a lack of understanding of the importance of financial reserves, poorly thought-through fund-raising events, the lack of a distinctive vision and mission, and a variety of other issues.

If you, as a leader, have a deficient background and understanding of finance, it is imperative that you acquire these competencies. Being financially competent will give you the ability to view your not-for-profit organization with a more comprehensive understanding of its overall functioning. It will give you a feeling of greater confidence as a leader. Financial competence will enable you to relate more effectively with your board of directors which is frequently composed of a number of business people. It will also enable you to better demonstrate how your organization is providing real value for the resources that have been provided to it. Having financial competence and understanding will help you to keep your job and thereby increase your contributions to your organization and the services it is providing to its constituents.

Financial competency for the "Observant Leader" is not an option. It is a necessary prerequisite to being a successful leader in smaller not-for-profit organizations which are, in many cases, under continuing financial stress.

Warning Signal
No. 12
Lack of Volunteer Involvement

Many smaller not-for-profit organizations involve volunteers in their efforts to achieve their missions. In fact, many smaller not-for-profits could not exist without the assistance of their volunteers. If you, as the leader of a smaller not-for-profit organization, fail to recognize the value that volunteers can bring to your organization, you may be seriously limiting the future success of your organization. You need to ask yourself the question, "Why you are not utilizing this valuable resource to augment and enhance the current resources that you have at your disposal?"

Common reasons for not utilizing the power of volunteer involvement are a lack of understanding of the potential of volunteers, a fear of lack of control, and a concern about the time and effort required to lead and manage volunteers.

It is a warning signal if you, as the leader of a smaller not-for-profit organization, have not carefully considered the potential of volunteer involvement in your organization. Possible advantages of involving volunteers are: being able to afford to increase the size of your workforce, acquiring job competencies that would not otherwise be available to you, adding role models of commitment that will inspire your paid employees, adding people who can serve as two-way communication links between your not-for-profit organization and the communities you serve of which they are members, having individuals in your organization who demonstrate through their behavior the importance of non-monetary motivators in energizing your workforce, having individuals in your organization who do not feel threatened in providing you with honest, open accurate feedback because they are not financially dependent upon your organization.

Regarding a concern about the time and effort required to lead and manage the volunteer effort along with a possible loss of control of this effort, some suggestions follow for maximizing the contributions of volunteers to your organization and its mission.

Suggestions for Leading and Managing Volunteers in Your Organization

- Create the position of coordinator of volunteers as either a paid or volunteer position to lead and manage the volunteer effort.
- Treat volunteers as full-fledged employees of your organization.
- Stress the importance of volunteers in helping your organization to achieve its mission.
- Hold joint sessions of volunteer and paid staff employees focusing on the best ways to work together.
- Determine what each volunteer hopes to get out of the volunteer experience.
- Develop a description for each of the volunteer positions.
- Develop a system of recognition for the achievements of volunteers.
- Create a culture of appreciation in your organization for the efforts of volunteers.
- Encourage feedback from volunteers concerning ways to improve your organization and the services it provides.
- Make it possible for each of your volunteers to have a mentor within your organization.
- Establish a system of feedback for volunteers concerning their performance.
- Include information about the importance of volunteers and their contributions to your organization in the information which is displayed about your organization.

CHAPTER 2

Problems with the Mission

"If you, as a leader, want the people in your organization to 'think big,' to exceed the expectations of your customers, your organization must know what business it is in, who your customers are, and how you can best serve them."

Problems with the Mission

Warning Signal
No. 1
The Mission and its Implementation is Not Different and Better

The mission of a smaller not-for-profit organization is of central importance. Mission deals with purpose. Achieving its mission is the ongoing reason for the existence of a not for profit organization. Unlike a for-profit organization, its purpose is not to make a profit. Nor is it a public sector governmental organization which is created to serve some segment or segments of the general public. The not-for-profit organization is a private non-governmental organization governed by a usually unpaid volunteer Board of Directors.

If a smaller not-for-profit organization is to be successful, it is of critical importance that the implementation of its mission be done in a manner that is distinctive and compelling. The mission must be important and have a real impact for the better in improving the aspect of the human condition which is the reason for its existence. If smaller not-for-profits are to have a significant impact their efforts must be focused on the specific target areas which are their areas of specialization. They need to be different, creative, and better. They need to be able to act quickly with agility and creativity building upon their strengths to meet emerging societal needs in their areas of specialization. The beliefs, values, and assumptions which motivate and drive these organizations should be evident in their mission statements and the manner in which they are implemented. The "character" of the organization should be readily observable.

The mission of the organization should be a motivator for all aspects of smaller not-for-profit organizations. The leader, Board, employees, and various constituents of the organization should be inspired by its importance in improving the lives of its clients and customers.

It is a warning signal for you, as the leader of a smaller not-for-profit organization, if the mission of your organization is not differentiated in its conceptualization and implementation. Is your organization really different and better as viewed by your constituents? Is your mission important and compelling? Is your organization really distinctive? If the answer is no, then you, as a leader, need to energize the forces within your organization that will build a culture that supports such a differentiated image and reality. Look to the present strengths of your organization and build upon them. Emphasize and communicate concerning the unique characteristics of your not-for-profit organization and watch it flourish.

Warning Signal
No. 2
The Mission Statement Does Not Clearly State What Business Your Organization is in, Who Your Customers are, and How You Will Serve Them

The author of this book, as a practitioner in the field, has found the writing of Ted Levitt of the Harvard Business School to be especially important and useful in thinking about organizational mission. In his ground breaking article entitled "Marketing Myopia" which is a classic in the field of Marketing, professor Levitt suggests that many people in business don't really understand what business they are in, and if they do, they define it too narrowly.

In order to develop a clear, relevant, and significant mission statement the leader of a smaller not-for-profit organization has to know what business his or her organization is really in. It is impossible to be clear and to the point if one doesn't understand the true nature of one's business. This is a major reason why so many mission statements are unfocused, convoluted, and unnecessarily complex. In many cases the person reading the mission statement finds it to be confusing and of little help in understanding the real purpose of the organization.

In addition to explaining the ongoing purpose of the organization the mission statement needs to identify who the customers of the organization are and how they will be served. How will your smaller not-for-profit organization have an impact for the better on the quality of the lives of the people and organizations being served? How will your organization do this in ways which are different and better?

Your mission statement should challenge everyone in your organization to work to the best of their abilities in achieving the goals of the organization. It should energize the members of your not-for-profit organization to "think big." If you, as a leader, want the people in your organization to "think big," to exceed the expectations of your customers, your organization must know what business it is in, who your customers are, and how you can best serve them.

It is a warning signal to you, as the "Observant Leader" if you find that there is confusion in your organization concerning the business you are in, the customers you would like to serve, and the manner in which you would like to serve them. Clarity of understanding throughout your organization concerning these three issues is essential if your organization is to be successful.

Warning Signal
No. 3
Your Organization is Not Living its Mission

The "Observant Leader" keeps asking the question- is our organization living its mission statement? Are we exhibiting our core values in the ways we behave? Are we walking the talk? If we say that we value our customers do we act in ways that clearly demonstrate that this is the case? Are the beliefs, values, assumptions and norms expressed in our mission statement demonstrated in our actions? Do the culture and the subcultures of our smaller not-for-profit organization support and sustain our mission? Does my behavior as the leader of the organization set an example for the behavior of the other members of my organization? Is my commitment to the mission of the organization inspiring the commitment of others? Are we working together to make our mission statement a powerful living document?

It is important for the "Observant Leader" to remember that if there is a conflict between what people say and what they do that what they do usually has much greater impact on the organization. In order for the mission or purpose of the organization to truly come alive it is the actions that really matter.

With regard to actions that are required to implement the mission on a consistent continuing basis it is important that smaller not-for-profit organizations hold regular interactive meetings of their staff, including their volunteers. It is easy for leaders of smaller not-for-profits to fall into a trap regarding the holding of such meetings. Because of the relative informality of these organizations there can be a tendency for the leader to rely on one to one interaction with individual members of the organization to get input about how the organization is performing with regard to its mission. Since these organizations are smaller the leader assumes that individuals are well informed about what is happening in the organization. The leader believes that he or she is getting comprehensive feedback about the accomplishment of mission related goals but is, in fact, not receiving the input that comes from the interaction of all or groups of people in the organization. The group interaction that is important in assessing movement toward the completion of mission directed goals is missing. The smaller not-for-profit organization is missing the great advantage that it has because of its smaller size to gather together the entire organization to hear differing views about what is happening and what actions need to be taken to keep the organization on track in achieving its mission. Accurate feedback is greatly facilitated by listening to different perspectives and points of view.

Such diversity of feedback is essential in accurately assessing how well your organization is achieving its mission. As the "Observant Leader" don't be lulled into the practice of relying upon individual feedback which is frequently limited to your friends and people with whom you agree, and of failing to get interactive feedback from the members of your organization as a group.

The "Observant Leader" creates opportunities for the employees of the organization to participate in a variety of activities that involve "living" the mission of the organization.

Participation is a powerful way of increasing motivation and commitment to living the mission on a day to day basis. Participation that involves direct contact with the recipients of the organization's services is especially powerful in motivating commitment to mission.

A major responsibility of the "Observant Leader" is to make the organization aware of gaps between its actions and its stated mission and to lead the charge to close these gaps in order to create a culture that truly supports and sustains the mission of the organization.

Warning Signal
No. 4
Your Mission Does Not Impact the Heart and the Mind

It is extremely important that the mission of your smaller not-for-profit organization have an emotional as well as an intellectual impact. People need to both feel and believe that what your organization is doing is of real importance. They must have an emotional as well as an intellectual connection with your organizational mission if they are to believe in it and be strongly committed to it. This is true for your employees, the people you serve, your supporters and donors, and the general public. If this is not the case, you, as the "Observant Leader," need to determine how you can relate what you are doing to both the intellect and the emotions of these groups and individuals.

Demonstrating the impact of the work your organization is doing to improve the lives of the people you are serving is critical to developing both an intellectual and emotional commitment to your mission. Personal stories about how the lives of the recipients of your organization's services have been improved are especially effective in communicating the importance of the work you are doing. Involving the recipients of your services in telling these stories is a highly desirable part of this process. It is one thing to talk about what your organization is doing in a general sense and quite another thing to hear personal stories told by the individuals who are directly affected. It is these personal stories relating to real life situations that communicate the emotional as well as the intellectual side of the organizational mission.

As has been emphasized previously in this book, the work of the not-for-profit organization is to improve some aspect of the human condition. Communicating about improvements in the human condition by its very nature, involves communicating on both an intellectual and emotional level if it is to have real impact.

As the "Observant Leader," it is important that you closely examine the emotional as well as the intellectual impact of your mission in order to be certain that it is perceived as important, powerful, worthwhile and deserving of support.

Warning Signal
No. 5
You are Not Reporting Your Mission Related Activities and Successes with Appropriate Frequency

One of the best Chamber of Commerce presidents that the author has observed is a master of reporting on past, present, and future events of his Chamber. He is able to generate a sense of great energy, success, and movement toward the goals of his Chamber of Commerce through this provision of frequent and continuing communication about the achievements of his organization. This frequent ongoing communication about the mission oriented work that is being done is important in creating momentum that moves the organization forward in achieving its goals and objectives.

Many not-for-profit organizations provide more intangible services rather than concrete products to their customers. It is of critical importance that they transform these intangible services into concrete results as perceived by their various constituents. In order to do this they have to keep reminding people what they have accomplished in the past, what they are presently accomplishing, and what they hope to accomplish in the future. They need to make intangibles tangible.

The "Observant Leader" pays close attention to this ongoing communication process about organizational activities and successes. This cannot be a hit or miss process. The "Observant Leader" knows that the organization must "blow its own horn." Its constituents have to know what it is doing. There has to be a strong sense of momentum that is built upon the achievement of goals and communication about these successes.

One of the important side effects of the frequent reporting of mission related activities and successes is the fact that such reporting serves to keep the organization on track in dealing with important issues. Individuals in the organization are encouraged to focus their energies on important and relevant mission oriented concerns rather than less important non-mission oriented issues. As mentioned previously in this book, it is easy for people in smaller not-for-profit organizations with limited staffing and other resources to be overwhelmed by pressing non-mission oriented tasks which divert them from the work that they need to do to accomplish the outcomes necessary to achieve their mission. It is the job of the "Observant Leader" to keep his or her organization on track.

The personal success of the leader as well as the success of his or her organization is often based on a perception of the momentum of the organization toward achieving its mission. If you, as the leader of a smaller not-for-profit organization, want to keep your job, it is essential that you pay close attention to the momentum exhibited by your organization in moving toward the completion of its goals. Does your organization project an image and a reality of moving ahead with confidence and energy as it works to achieve its goals? Is it perceived as a dynamic organization? Are you, as the leader, communicating about the successes you are achieving in an understandable manner? Is your frequent and consistent communication about what you are doing stimulating feedback from the recipients of this communication? Do people really appreciate the importance of the work your organization is doing? Frequent ongoing high impact communication about your organization's activities and successes is of critical importance in creating such an understanding as well as an increased interest in and support of the work your organization is doing.

CHAPTER 3

Problems with the Board

"Among the threats to maintaining an adequate organizational reserve fund are board members who embark on non-mission related ego oriented activities that drain the organization's finances."

Problems with the Board

Warning Signal
No. 1
Board Members Who Do Not Understand Their Roles and Responsibilities and Act Inappropriately

In the author's experience as a practitioner in not for profit organizations the most frequent violation of Board member behavior regarding roles and responsibilities takes place in direct interactions with employees. These interactions occur when Board members become involved in the operational side of managerial functions. These ventures of Board members into the operational side of managing the organization tend to fall into two areas of direct interpersonal contact with employees.

The first is to talk to employees in different parts of the organization and give them orders and directives about how to do specific jobs. They act as if they are the direct supervisor of the employees with whom they are interacting. They believe that since they are Board members they have the authority to go around telling employees how to do their jobs.

The second problem area of direct Board member-employee interaction occurs when Board members encourage employees to come directly to them to discuss and resolve difficulties in their jobs and work performance rather than taking these issues to their immediate supervisor. The informal culture of many smaller not-for-profit organizations can sometimes encourage this direct interaction with Board members as employees can more easily get to know Board members and come to perceive them as personal friends. As the "Observant Leader," you need to be aware that these direct interactions between your Board members and employees can be extremely upsetting to members of your supervisory staff. Having their authority undercut by the actions of Board members can cause real morale problems and seriously affect the sense of teamwork in your organization. Immediate action must be taken to see to it that the Board member involved instructs the employee in question to direct his concerns to his immediate supervisor. In cases where the behavior of a Board member drifts into the operational side of the leadership function it is a wise leader who proactively involves the Board Chair in discussions with the Board member. The importance of acting quickly in cases of Board members acting as if they were paid managerial employees cannot be emphasized enough. If these situations are allowed to fester the displeasure of supervisory employees having their authority undercut by Board members can easily be redirected to you as the leader.

Another area of Board member behavior which involves an inappropriate understanding of Board roles and responsibilities has to do with the involvement of Board members in the hiring process. It is a warning signal if you, as the leader of a smaller not-for-profit organization, find that members of your Board want to become directly involved in the hiring process of the employees who are working for you as paid employees. You, as the leader, are responsible for deciding which new employees will be hired or recommended to be hired. Being in charge of the hiring process is of critical importance to your success. Don't allow Board members to take this responsibility away from you. It is an observation of the author of this book that leaders who allow Board intervention in the hiring process of their employees are probably on their way out as leaders of their organizations. A leader has to be able to control the hiring process.

Leadership is a team effort and the selection of this team is an essential ingredient for success. If you, as a leader of a smaller not-for-profit organization, lose the ability to hire the people you want, it is probably time for you to move on to lead another organization. The "Observant Leader" knows that identifying and hiring the right people in the first place is essential in building the foundation for continuing success in the future.

Warning Signal
No. 2
The Board is Large and the Executive Committee is Ambitious

Some smaller not-for-profit organizations have very large Boards. If this is the case in your not-for-profit organization you, as "Observant Leader," need to keep a careful eye on the relationship between the full Board and the Executive Committee. It is a warning signal to you if the Executive Committee attempts to take over the Board decision making process and begins to make decisions that should involve the full Board. A key person in this relationship between the Executive Committee and the full Board is the Board Chair. The Chair has to see to it that all the members of the Board have the opportunity to participate as fully functioning members and not have their functions as Board members circumvented by overly ambitious members of the Executive Committee. Board members who find that they are being shut out of their rightful roles as Board members by an overly energetic and ambitious executive committee are probably not going to be happy people. This displeasure can easily become directed at you, as the paid leader of the organization.

Executive Committee members may become overly involved in the work of the full Board for what they believe are good reasons. They may feel that the large size of your Board makes it unusually cumbersome and inefficient. They may be right, but that does not justify taking over functions that should be handled by the full Board. It is up to you, as the organization's leader, working with the Board Chair to see to it that this does not happen. It may be necessary to re-organize the structure of the Board or to reduce it in size. However this may not be possible because of a need to adequately represent the organization's constituents on the Board or a legal or legislative requirement that certain groups or individuals be included. A smaller Board may eliminate the need for frequent meetings of an executive committee. The author of this book is an advocate of smaller Boards for smaller not-for-profit organizations consisting ideally of seven or nine members.

Warning Signal
No. 3
Board Members Who Are Largely Self-Serving Rather than Mission-Serving

Board members who are largely self-serving rather than mission-serving can be a big problem for you as a leader of a smaller not-for-profit organization.

Self-serving Board members appear in many different forms. They may be "false friends," individuals with big egos, users of your organization to advance their professional or political careers, or other individuals with a variety of vested interests other than helping you and your organization achieve your mission. Self-serving Board members may also appear in a variety of other disguises that can do considerable damage to you personally as well as to your organization.

These self-serving Board members undermine the spirit and morale of your organization taking focus away from the mission of your organization. They frequently create distrust, friction, and a sense of unease in the organization. These self-serving Board members can undermine the effectiveness of your leadership by undermining the teamwork and group cohesiveness of your Board and your organization.

It is of the upmost importance that the Board selection process focus on the reasons that the interested person would like to become a member of the Board. Is this individual really motivated to help your organization accomplish its mission? Is the potential

Board member willing to make a serious effort to help your organization achieve its goals? The Board of a smaller not-for-profit organization cannot afford to have Board members who are primarily interested in pursuing their own self oriented agendas. These self-serving applicants for your Board need to be identified prior to their consideration for Board membership. It is important that you, as the leader, be a part of this screening process. Smaller not-for-profit organizations can ill afford to bring individuals on to the Board who are not prepared to give a strong commitment to their work.

As mentioned previously, smaller not-for-profits have a smaller margin for error in the decisions they are required to make in order to be successful. They require superior performance by their Boards if they are to successfully cope with the many challenges that they face in successfully accomplishing their missions.

A major responsibility of the "Observant Leader" in smaller not-for-profit organizations is to see to it that there is a strong individual and team commitment to the mission of the organization that takes precedence over personally oriented vested interests. Individual Board members must be shown that it is possible for them to best achieve their personal goals by being a member of a winning mission oriented team. Mission serving Board members serve as important role models for the organization as a whole. Cooperation and teamwork are emphasized rather than self-interest and self-aggrandizement.

Another responsibility of the "Observant Leader" is to identify and recommend potential mission oriented members to the Board. The leader's relationship with the Board Chair and the Board Nominating Committee is of particular importance in this regard. You, as the leader, are in an ideal position to evaluate how potential Board members would be able to contribute both to the Board and to the overall organization. You should also be able to evaluate how well you would be able to work with these individuals in their roles as Board members. As the leader of your not-for-profit organization you should be proactive in working diligently with the Board Chair and Nominating Committee to build and develop a Board that puts the mission of the organization above personal self-interest. It is important for the "Observant Leader" to remember that it is far more difficult to convert self-serving Board members into mission-serving Board members than it is to bring mission-serving individuals on to the Board in the first place.

The "Observant Leader" knows that self-serving Board members can undermine the morale of the Board and the entire organization. They can also be a real threat to the success and survival of the leader. This is especially the case in smaller not-for-profit organizations where the friction and unease created by self-serving individuals can be readily observed and be especially devastating.

Board membership should be a win-win relationship involving the individual Board member, the entire Board, the leader and administrative team, and the organization as a whole. The individual Board member should grow from the experience as he or she contributes to achieving the organizational mission.

It is the belief of the author that the best way to relate to a largely self-serving Board member is to meet with the individual and the Board Chair and make every effort to find out what that individual is attempting to gain from being a member of the Board. With an understanding of the Board member's personal agenda in mind, the goal is then to determine how you, as the leader, along with the Board Chair, can create a situation where the Board member involved can achieve his or her personal goals as part of the process of achieving the organization's goals.

The objective is to align the Board member's personal goals with the organization's goals thereby strengthening his or her commitment to the mission of the organization. It is important that you, as the leader, involve the Board Chair throughout this process. This is another example of the central importance of the Leader-Board Chair relationship in successfully leading a smaller not-for-profit organization.

Warning Signal
No. 4
Board Members Who Do Not Understand and Appreciate the Complexity of a Smaller Not-For-Profit Organization and the Difficulty of the Leadership Job

Historically and to a certain extent there still exists the idea that private sector organizations are far more difficult to lead and manage than not-for-profit organizations. It was considered a startling revelation in some quarters when Peter Drucker expressed the view that it is more difficult to lead and manage a not-for-profit organization than a private sector or public sector organization.

If members of your Board believe that your job as the leader of a smaller not-for-profit organization is a "piece of cake" this could present a real problem for you in terms of the encouragement, support, respect, and financial compensation that you receive from them.

In addition to not being aware of and understanding the complexities of smaller not-for-profit organizations there are two related factors which are identified below, that sometimes diminish Board member perception of the value and difficulty of the leadership position in smaller not-for-profit organizations. They are the fact that Board members usually do not receive financial compensation for their services and also that in many cases they are employed in the private sector.

The fact that a Board member is not being paid financially but is doing important and sometimes time consuming work for the organization can cause the Board member to ask herself why the paid leader of the organization is receiving as much compensation as is the case. The question in the mind of the Board member is- I'm doing the work for no pay, why should the leader receive as much money as she is getting? In addition, the Board member says, "After all this is a not-for-profit organization and the money should be going to the organization's clients not to paying our employees." It is the author's view that paying the leader and staff of smaller not-for-profit organizations a respectable salary and thereby attracting competent people will result in more benefits being received by the organization's clients than paying inadequate salaries and hiring less competent people. A high level of leadership, managerial, and organizational competence is required if smaller not-for-profit organizations are to deal successfully with the complex demands of operating a small organization which is almost always vulnerable to sudden changes in its internal and external environments.

The fact that many Board members work in for-profit organizations can also cause potential problems for you, as the leader of a smaller not-for-profit organization. The culture of a business organization can be quite different from the culture of a not-for-profit organization. The profit motive is obviously of great importance in the private sector. Without a profit the organization can't continue to exist. The purpose of not-for-profit organizations is to achieve their missions, not to make a profit. It may be difficult for private sector employees on Boards of not-for-profit organizations to understand and appreciate these differences. If the Board members work in a large private sector organization the culture of the smaller not-for-profit organization may be even more difficult to understand.

If you, as a leader of a smaller not-for-profit organization, want your Board to understand and appreciate the challenges of dealing with the complex demands of your organization, it is imperative that you communicate on a regular basis about the nature of these challenges. The Board's participation in identifying and successfully meeting these challenges should result in building support for and an appreciation of your work and the work of the leadership team. It should foster an attitude of mutual respect, support, commitment, and trust between the Board and the leadership team. Appreciating the challenges involved in achieving the organization's mission should help to make it evident that the goals of the organization can only be achieved if both the Board and the leadership team support each other. The Board should want the leader and the leadership team to be successful and the leader and the leadership team should want the Board to be successful. This attitude of "Let's work together to achieve great things," is of the greatest importance if you, as the leader are to survive and flourish in your job.

The Difficulty and Complexity of Leading a Not-For-Profit Organization

Why are smaller not-for-profit organizations especially complex?

- They frequently have undependable funding sources which are unpredictable.
- They are often dependent to some degree on financial and other support from the public sector.
- They are often dependent to some degree on financial and other support from the private sector.
- They frequently lead and manage volunteers who are not paid financially by the organization.
- They have volunteers on their committees which they supervise who also serve on the governing Boards of their organizations.
- They must gain the support of a diverse group of individuals who serve as members of their governing Boards.
- Since they deal largely with intangible services it is more difficult to measure the extent of their successes in achieving their mission related goals.
- They most likely have limited human resources.
- They most likely lack certain important managerial competencies, equipment, and knowledge which they require assistance in acquiring.

- The difficulty of their leadership and management tasks is not recognized and appreciated.
- They cannot afford to have poor performing employees. Each employee must carry his or her own weight. They cannot hide poor performance.
- They must develop and sustain a unique identity in order to survive.
- They must be creative and innovative in their areas of expertise if they are to survive.
- They must be different and better.
- They have a smaller margin for error in the decisions they make.
- They cannot afford to have periods of poor or average performance. They must "be on their game" on a continuing basis. Their level of success can change very rapidly.

Warning Signal
No. 5
Board Members Who Do Not Understand that Smaller Not-For-Profit Organizations Are Frequently Financially Vulnerable

It is a warning signal to the "Observant Leader" when members of the Board demonstrate that they do not understand that smaller not-for-profit organizations are frequently financially vulnerable. There are a number of reasons for this financial vulnerability. These include susceptibility to changes in the economy, unpredictability of funding sources, lack of economy of scale, inadequate financial reserves, unpredictability of the number of available volunteers, lack of control of overhead costs, having to operate in inadequate facilities, and gaps in managerial expertise.

There are four warning signals in particular that the author of this book would like to call to your attention as the "Observant Leader" concerning ways in which Board members fail to understand the financial vulnerability of smaller not-for-profit organizations.

The first warning signal is when the Board fails to recognize the importance of having adequate financial reserves. Building and maintaining adequate financial reserves is an important Board responsibility. The Board is responsible for the financial well-being of the organization. It has to decide what the proper level of financial reserves is for the organization within the context of its mission and its ability to function at an optimal level.

An adequate financial reserve provides a sense of security that enables the members of the organization to focus on carrying out the organizational mission rather than spending their time worrying about whether or not the organization will survive. Ongoing financial insecurity is not conducive to creating an environment where the organization serves its clients with excellence.

It is therefore important that the Board keep a careful watch on the level of financial reserves as an important part of its financial oversight of the organization. The "Observant Leader" should also pay close attention to the level of the financial reserves.

Among the threats to maintaining an adequate organizational reserve fund are Board members who embark on non-mission related ego oriented activities that drain the organization's finances. It is not uncommon for some Board members to attempt to institute projects which will improve their public image and advance their careers at the expense of the organization.

In addition to the financial problems which such ventures create, they also consume the valuable time of employees which is badly needed to successfully complete mission oriented projects. The "Observant Leader," working closely with the Chairman of the Board, needs to see to it that these ego centered activities do not receive the support of the Board. The "Observant Leader" needs to be on the lookout for these ego driven projects that severely undermine the work of the organization. In smaller not-for-profit organizations ego oriented non-mission related projects can be a big problem. It is important that the "Observant Leader" diligently work to attempt to change these ego oriented ventures into mission oriented initiatives.

Poorly thought through fundraisers are another threat to the financial well-being of smaller not-for-profit organizations. Many smaller not-for-profit organizations depend on a variety of fundraising events to achieve balanced budgets. Dependence on fundraisers to balance the budget is another part of the vulnerability of smaller not-for-profit organizations. Fundraisers should be mission-oriented whenever possible. If they are not directly mission related, there is almost always the opportunity to communicate how the money being raised is helping the organization involved achieve its goals. A warning signal to the "Observant Leader" appears when there is not significant interest and support for the project. Fundraisers that have the support of only a few individuals frequently turn out to be a minor or major disaster. Fundraising ideas should be carefully considered and approved by the full Board before being implemented. Fundraisers should not only provide resources, but they should also clarify and enhance the image of the not-for-profit organization.

Poorly planned and run fundraisers can be a serious problem for smaller not-for-profit organizations who cannot afford to have financial disasters. They can also cost you your job as the leader of a smaller not-for-profit organization.

Another threat to the financial well-being of smaller not-for-profit organizations is the tendency of some Board members to want to give some of their organization's financial resources to other organizations or causes which they think are deserving of support. Someone from another organization may approach a member of your Board with an appeal for financial assistance. Your board member thinks it would be a nice thing to do to help this organization out. The organization in question most likely has little or nothing to do with the purpose of your organization except in a very general sense. Your Board member may not understand how financially vulnerable your organization is as a smaller not-for-profit organization. He or she may not realize that the financial health of a smaller not-for-profit organization can change very rapidly. It is your responsibility as the "Observant Leader" to keep a close eye on proposals that are made by members of your Board to "help out" "needy organizations." The Board Chair has an important role to play as a "watch dog" to see that the scarce resources of your organization are not frittered away on endeavors that are not related to your mission as a not-for-profit organization. The resources of your organization need to be conserved and used for the purposes for which your organization was created.

CHAPTER 4

Problems within the Organization

"It cannot be stressed enough that it is imperative that you understand the workings of the informal organization and its relationship to the formal organization that appears on the organization chart."

Problems within the Organization

Warning Signal
No. 1
Lack of Employee Pride and Commitment to Being Different and Better

A theme that has been given major attention in previous books of the author has been the necessity for not-for-profit organizations to be different and better. The author owes a deep debt of gratitude to Ferd Ensinger, a brilliant management consultant, for introducing him to the critical importance of creating organizations that have a uniqueness about them that makes them different and better.

As you, as the "Observant Leader," look around at your smaller not-for-profit organization it is important that you carefully check on the level of pride and commitment that your employees have in the uniqueness and quality of their organization. Are they truly committed to achieving the mission of the organization in creative and innovative ways? Are they committed to being first in the minds of their customers and potential customers in their areas of service? Do they take pride in implementing new ideas and new approaches? Do they dare to be different from others as they continue to create an organization that is unique and better? Do they have the courage not to be like everyone else? Do they experience a pride of ownership?

Your job as the "Observant Leader" is to support and encourage your employees in their efforts to be different and better. Smaller not-for-profit organizations usually provide services to specific groups of potential customers. They frequently do not have the resources to serve broad based large constituencies. They have to focus and maximize their resources to their greatest benefit in serving somewhat specific audiences. In these areas of service they have to be different and better if they are to be successful on a continuing basis. They have to use their smaller size, which has the advantage of being less bureaucratic and more agile, to respond quickly to meet the changing needs of their customer base and stay in the forefront of their areas of service. Smaller not-for-profit organizations have to know what they do best and continue to build on these strengths. They need to know what they want to be known for and take pride in being first in the minds of the communities they serve in their areas of expertise.

Warning Signal
No. 2
Deficiencies in the "Feeling" of the Organization

Excellent smaller not-for-profit organizations have a "feeling" about them that gives one a sense of competence, energy, commitment, health, and high performance. If your smaller not-for-profit organization is lacking in these important attributes it is a warning signal that action is required to work to improve these important organizational qualities. To be successful in achieving their missions with the limited resources available to them, these organizations need to excel in the characteristics mentioned above.

Following are some aspects of the "feeling" level of your organization that you, as the "Observant Leader," need to carefully consider and provide appropriate leadership to strengthen if they are found to be in need of improvement.

As The "Observant Leader" Ask Yourself the Following Questions

Do the members of my organization?:

- Demonstrate a strong commitment to the mission of the organization?
- Exhibit a sense of pride in the work they are doing?
- Trust each other and the way in which the organization operates based on its values and beliefs.
- Exhibit energy and enthusiasm concerning the work they are doing.
- Enjoy what they are doing. Are they having any fun?
- Work well as a team. Is there a spirit of cooperation and good feeling?
- Value and exhibit creativity and innovation in their work.
- Experience a sense of personal achievement and personal growth in their work.
- Have a good level of morale.
- Participate in a proactive manner in addressing new challenges relating to their work.

How does the "Observant Leader" get a realistic and accurate picture of the "feeling" of the organization which he or she leads? The author of this book believes that it is essential that the leader go out into the organization and interact on a personal basis with his or her employees. Despite the power and importance of electronic communication of all kinds, the leader has to "go out" to be with his people from time to time. A big advantage of smaller not-for-profit organizations is that the smaller size of the organization should make this kind of personal interaction easier to accomplish with greater frequency.

An example of the importance of getting out to be with the people is illustrated by the story of a friend of the author of this book who had recently secured ownership of a new company. The new owner, an extremely successful entrepreneur of other businesses, believed strongly in getting out into the organization and talking to the employees in order to receive first-hand feedback from them concerning their feelings about the company. The owner discovered that there was considerable dissatisfaction among the workers of the company he had just acquired because the management personnel were receiving free donuts but this benefit was not being received by the non-management employees. The situation was changed so that all the employees, management and non-management, received free donuts. This seemingly small matter might not have been discovered if the new owner had not gone out into the workplace to get to know his employees and learn how they felt about various issues. The morale in his new workplace was improved by his going out into the workplace, listening, and taking what he considered to be appropriate action.

It is important in the process of attempting to get balanced and accurate feedback about the "feeling" level of your smaller not-for-profit organization not to fall into the practice of talking only to individuals. Because your organization is smaller you may believe that each individual is well informed about what is happening in the overall organization or represents the thinking of his or her fellow employees. The fact may be that the individual you are talking to may not know what is really going on in your organization and may not be an accurate gauge of what other people are thinking. Make every effort to talk not only to individuals but also to small groups and to the organization as a whole. Group interaction may give you, as the "Observant Leader," insights into the "feeling" of the organization that you would not receive when talking to individuals.

In receiving communication feedback about the "feeling" level of your organization don't talk only to people who are your friends or agree with the goals you are pursuing for your organization. Communicate also with people of differing perspectives and points of view. Talk to individuals and groups with different types of responsibilities who do different kinds of work.

Remember, you are attempting to get an accurate and balanced understanding of the way people in your organization feel about it and their personal satisfaction or lack of it as a result of being a part of it. Security personnel, custodians, and food services workers are often a valuable resource for receiving input about the "feeling" of employees in your organization as they interact with many of them on an informal basis.

It is important not to accept "they say" kinds of feedback from individuals in your organization as being accurate and balanced concerning the feelings of your employees at face value.

Statements such as "they say morale is low," "they say most of our employees feel that they are in jobs with no future," or "they say that our employees are fed up with high management salaries" should be considered initially as the remarks of one individual and then investigated to determine the extent to which they are accurate.

In assessing the "feeling" level of your smaller not-for-profit organization it is important to encourage and reward suggestions from your employees for making your workplace more personally satisfying. What do they like the best about working for your organization and what suggestions do they have for making it better?

The "feeling" level of a smaller not-for-profit organization as viewed by the "Observant Leader" is based on both fact and intuition. Although the "feeling" level of an organization is to some degree intangible this does not mean that it is unimportant. The energy, sense of pride, creative and innovative spirit, level of trust, good feeling and teamwork, present or not present in an organization are related to the outcomes it achieves. Successful organizations project a feeling of success, competence, and vitality. Successful organizations feel alive and purposeful.

It is important to remember that your not-for-profit organization is in the human improvement business. It should also be in the business of providing an environment for your employees that is "growth producing" for them.

To be at their best, your employees have to project a competent, helpful, cheerful, caring attitude that is supported by the helpful, caring, optimistic environment in which they work.

It is a warning signal to the "Observant Leader" if there is a lack of excitement and energy in his or her smaller not-for-profit organization. It is a warning signal if there is not a creative and innovative spirit. Smaller not-for-profit organizations because of their size, greater informality, sense of community, and greater opportunity for face-to-face communication have the capacity and opportunity to use these factors to create a "feeling" level in their organizations that inspires confidence in their ability to be successful.

Warning Signal
No. 3
Lack of Managerial and Other Job Competencies

A serious problem that smaller not-for-profit organizations frequently face is being able to hire an adequate number of employees and to acquire specialists with first rate skills and competencies. They do not have the financial resources to meet their personnel requirements. What they do about this situation becomes of critical importance to them in leading their organizations. The author of this book believes strongly that a cardinal rule with regard to hiring people for smaller not-for-profits is to not settle for average or below average people. It is his view that it is better to have fewer people of a higher caliber than to have more people of lesser ability and motivation. Poor performers with inadequate competencies can be a serious problem for you as the leader of a smaller not-for-profit organization. This is especially true of people in financial positions in your organization where competence and trust are of critical importance. It is a warning signal of major proportions if your financial people demonstrate incompetence or lack of trust. Such people can cost you your job! It is important to remember that financial difficulties are a major reason for leaders of smaller not-for-profit organizations losing their jobs.

Volunteers can prove to be a significant way to remedy gaps in the workforce of smaller not-for-profit organizations. Following are some suggestions for acquiring and utilizing volunteers in meeting the personnel requirements of smaller not-for-profit organizations.

These suggestions are: (1) stress the importance of the work being done in helping your organization achieve its mission, (2) treat volunteers as regular members of the staff, (3) create working situations that meet both the needs of the organization and the needs of the volunteer, and (4) recognize the importance of the work of volunteers in the overall success of the organization. The fact of the matter is that without the involvement of volunteers many smaller not-for-profit organizations could not survive.

With regard to the first suggestion there are almost always highly competent people around who excel in their regular jobs and professions looking for opportunities to contribute to important and worthwhile causes outside of their normal areas of employment. The "Observant Leader" needs to encourage efforts to alert these individuals to such opportunities in his or her organization.

The second suggestion of treating volunteers as regular members of the staff is extremely important. Volunteers should not be viewed as "second class citizens." They should be viewed as fully participating members of the organization. The fact that they are not being paid monetarily but are nevertheless highly motivated and highly committed to the work of the organization should be applauded and recognized. They should be expected to perform at a high-level as is true of the other members of the organization and be held accountable for their performance.

With regard to the third suggestion for successfully integrating volunteers into the workforce of smaller not-for-profit organizations, work situations must be created to allow volunteers to contribute their best efforts while meeting the requirements of the organization. Working hours, travel requirements, required continuity of effort, and other outside responsibilities must be considered. There must be mutual agreement between the volunteer and the organization concerning these matters if the involvement of the volunteer is to be satisfying and productive.

The fourth suggestion concerning the importance of the recognition of volunteers cannot be stressed enough. Volunteers are being paid in psychological and social ways. They are being paid in terms of their personal satisfaction in doing important work that helps to achieve important goals. In addition to the inner satisfaction they receive they should also be recognized by the organization and its members for the work they are doing. Such recognition is extremely important in motivating volunteers. The importance of volunteer involvement should be stressed in the publications and public communications of the organization. The recognition of volunteer involvement and contributions to the organization should be a major priority of the "Observant Leader."

Some key functions and responsibilities in smaller not-for-profit organizations may lend themselves with more or less success to being performed by volunteers.

Among these areas of responsibility are: financial management, fundraising, membership recruitment, technology implementation, systems development, and marketing and public relations. Issues of central concern when involving volunteers in major positions in these areas of responsibility are the issues of competence, motivation, and dependability.

An important position in creating an outstanding volunteer effort which is highly recommended by the author of this book is that of Coordinator of Volunteers. This position can be successfully performed by either a volunteer or a paid member of the staff depending upon the best fit for the particular organization involved. The job of the Coordinator of Volunteers is to provide support for the overall volunteer effort in the organization.

Achieving a strong volunteer effort requires careful attention and good planning. Fitting the right volunteer into the right position involves an understanding of the needs of the volunteer and the requirements of the position. This process requires a focused effort. The leader of smaller not-for-profit organizations is frequently faced with a range of responsibilities that do not allow for the necessary time required to do a great job in the volunteer leadership role. This is the reason that the Coordinator of Volunteers position can be of great assistance and value.

The Coordinator helps to organize the overall volunteer effort as well as working with the individual volunteer and the supervisor to whom the volunteer reports. The Coordinator of Volunteers does not directly supervise the volunteer. This is done by the supervisor who appears on the formal organization chart. The coordinator is a resource person, a facilitator, a planner, a motivator, and a champion for the volunteer effort in the smaller not-for-profit organization. Among the important jobs of the Coordinator is facilitating the working relationship between the volunteers and the paid staff. The Coordinator is involved in helping to create an appreciation of the importance of the volunteers and the paid staff working together to achieve outstanding results.

It cannot be stressed enough that the "Observant Leader" has to be directly involved with the employee hiring and selection process. This process is critical to the success of smaller not-for-profit organizations which cannot afford to make many mistakes in the selection and recruitment of new members of the organization. The "Observant Leader" has to insist that the organization not settle for second rate employees. Each person in smaller not-for-profit organizations must be able to perform at a superior level. There is no room for average or less than average performance. Employees are required who are generalists and employees are required who are specialists. Hopefully both of these qualities can be found in some of the individuals who are brought on board as members of the organization. The "Observant Leader" must give considerable thought to the job requirements of the organization, establish priorities, and lead the way to acquire the personnel that will get the job done with excellence.

Warning Signal
No. 4
Lack of Operating Systems

Smaller non-for profit organizations need to have systematic ways of doing things. These organizations do not have the personnel to deal with the large number of issues involved in running a smaller not-for-profit organization on an individual case to case basis. They have to have systems that take care of the majority of routine decisions. This allows the staff of the organization to spend their time and energy on important issues that really make a difference for their clients and customers. Reducing time spent on routine matters frees up the smaller not-for-profit organization to use its strengths of providing a warm, caring, humanistic, growth providing environment in support of things of the first importance. It is important to emphasize early in our discussion of systems that these systems should have built into them the opportunity for human intervention and decision making when such intervention is considered to be desirable. In creating systems one must carefully consider the need for both consistency in practice and the need to intervene if exceptions to normal practice are required.

Following is a listing of advantages that well thought through systems can provide for your smaller not-for-profit organization. In addition, there are suggestions provided regarding things to consider when creating these systems.

Advantages of Good Operating Systems for Smaller Not-For-Profit Organizations:

- Your services are available to a greater number of clients and customers.
- There is more time for members of your organization to deal with non-routine matters and decisions.
- There is increased consistency in serving your clients and customers.
- Services are provided on a regular ongoing basis rather than a "hit" or "miss" basis.
- Increases your ability to improve the quality of the services you provide.
- Increases your capacity to do research in a variety of areas.
- Enables you to share information more quickly and widely.
- Makes it possible for you to receive more feedback from your clients and customers.
- Enables you to improve and expand the flow of information you send to the communities you serve.

Things to Consider When Creating a Good Operating System:

- The purposes of the system.
- Designing a system that best achieves the purposes of the system.
- Appropriate ways to intervene if considered desirable.
- Consistency in practice.
- Simplicity- avoiding unnecessary complexity.
- Designing a system that is considerate of the people operating and using it.
- The ability to sustain the system.
- Visible benefits of the system for those operating and accessing it.
- A system that is humane.
- A system that relates to your other systems in an integrated manner and does not conflict with or duplicate them.

One of the major functions of operating systems is to monitor changes in the internal and external environments of the organization. In the internal environment changes in the level of morale, commitment to mission, productivity, and financial well-being are examples of the kinds of things that need to be monitored. In the external landscape some of the changes that need to be carefully watched are the economic and political environments, new initiatives of not-for-profit, private, and public sector organizations in your areas of service, present and potential donor priorities, customer satisfaction, and community and public support.

Operational systems that support ongoing research are very important to smaller not-for-profit organizations because they need to be leaders in implementing new ideas, concepts, and programs if they are to be successful. Don't fall into the trap that too many smaller not-for-profit organizations fall into of believing that they don't have time to do research. A failure to "stay ahead of the pack" can easily result in a smaller not-for-profit organization going out of business. As we have stated before, smaller not-for-profit organizations are frequently financially vulnerable because they have a smaller margin for error. In addition to developing and utilizing their own research capabilities, successful not-for-profit organizations know how to tap into the research sources of other not-for-profit, private, and public organizations by building partnerships with them.

It is important that smaller not-for-profit organizations build into their culture an appreciation on the part of each employee of the importance of research and the feedback that it provides. It is also important that each employee participate in the research and feedback process.

It is a warning signal for you, as the "Observant Leader," if your operating systems do not support your organization's ability to successfully meet the challenges and opportunities facing it. These operating systems should focus on areas of information and performance that will make your smaller not-for-profit organization different, better, and a leader in providing services and products that have a positive impact on the lives of the people being served.

Warning Signal
No. 5
Self-Serving Cliques

The author of this book is defining cliques as small groups of individuals who have certain characteristics in common, who identify with each other on some basis, who have certain common agendas, and who are usually somewhat exclusive with regard to individuals who are not members of the clique. The common characteristics of a clique may include such characteristics as age, ethnicity, schools attended, extent of education, social class background, professional training, and type of occupation.

The "Observant Leader" of a smaller not-for-profit organization needs to pay attention to the cliques that exist in his or her organization. These cliques can be helpful in the efforts of smaller not-for-profit organizations to achieve their missions or they can become a barrier to these efforts. Self-serving cliques can undermine the teamwork of your organization and become a disruptive force. Cliques can exist on the Board of Directors, on the leadership team, or in work groups throughout your organization.

It is important for you, as the "Observant Leader," to identify the leaders of these cliques and work with them to motivate their groups to move beyond their own vested interests to support the overall organization and its mission oriented goals. Cliques on the leadership team of your organization can be a special problem. It is not an uncommon situation for members of the leadership team to attempt to manipulate cliques in the organization to advance their own status, power, and vested interests.

Cliques represent one component of the informal relationships that exist within every organization. The informal organization does not appear on the formal organization chart but its power and influence in determining what happens in an organization can be highly significant. Cliques and other groups in the informal organization can be your ally or may prevent you from being the successful leader who can have a real impact for the better on your organization and its clients.

The smaller size of your not-for-profit organization should help you, as the "Observant Leader," to observe and educate yourself about the nature of your informal organization. It cannot be stressed enough that it is imperative that you understand the workings of the informal organization and its relationship to the formal organization that appears on the organization chart. As mentioned frequently in this book, smaller not-for-profit organizations need all the friends and supporters they can get. To be successful, you as the leader, need the broad based support of all the people in your organization not just the personnel who appear with titles on the formal organization chart.

The successful smaller not-for-profit organization is proactive in providing information and training to the leaders of cliques and other groups in the informal organization. The individuals who do not appear on the organization chart need to be recognized and rewarded for their contributions if a true sense of teamwork is to take place.

Transforming self serving cliques into goal directed mission oriented groups can be an important part of building employee teamwork and support for the mission throughout the organization.

Warning Signal
No. 6
An Overabundance of Rumors

In smaller not-for-profit organizations there is no excuse for employees not being well informed about what is happening regarding their organization. As the "Observant Leader" it is your responsibility to see to it that your employees are well informed concerning the results your organization is achieving, the steps that are being taken to improve performance, and present and future organizational priorities. There should be a minimum of rumors floating around the organization. The presence of a large number of rumors indicates that your employees are not being properly informed through the formal communication channels of your organization.

Rumors involve information being communicated through the grapevine which consists of the information channels of the informal organization. Rumors contain information which is inaccurate and misleading. They can travel throughout the organization in a very short period of time. Rumors about such issues as pending layoffs, upcoming mergers, loss of contracts, and pending legislation detrimental to the organization, can be very damaging to the morale of smaller not-for-profit organizations which are especially vulnerable to such events.

Smaller not-for-profit organizations should have an advantage over larger organizations in becoming aware of the existence of rumors and in being able to move quickly to counteract them because they are usually much less bureaucratic. The author of this book, based on personal experience as a practitioner in smaller not-for-profit organizations, suggests several ways in which rumors can be dealt with quickly and effectively.

The first is to get the entire organization together and discuss the specific rumors that have been circulating over the grapevine. Since the organization is small it may be quite possible to assemble the entire organization together in one place and have a face-to-face interactive session with all the employees that will eliminate misunderstanding about the issue at hand.

This may not be possible in smaller not-for-profits with larger numbers of employees. If this is the case, an interactive meeting of all the employees in the organization can be initiated through some form of appropriate electronic technology. There is sometimes a tendency in smaller not-for-profits to focus on one to one relationships with employees assuming that because of their smaller size the leader will be able to reach all employees throughout the organization using this one on one approach. The problem is that the interaction that occurs through group meetings is missing and issues are frequently not as carefully or thoroughly explored.

Another approach to dealing with rumors is to use the grapevine itself as the communication vehicle to provide accurate and current information. There are usually key members of any grapevine who are perceived as distributors of the information being communicated. The "Observant Leader" needs to be aware of these principal communicators in the grapevine and provide them with correct information to replace the information being transmitted through the rumors.

In addition, it is important that you, as the leader of the organization, see that changes are made to the formal communication channels used by your organization in order to provide timely and accurate feedback to your employees concerning issues of concern to them. Your employees must have information concerning their performance and the performance of the organization if they are to be highly motivated, productive, and satisfied employees.

Rumors can be very disruptive as they distort the reality of what is actually taking place in your organization. Rumors undermine the morale of your people because of the anxiety and false perceptions that they create.

As the "Observant Leader" you should use the inherent advantages of a smaller organization which are its agility, informality, lack of bureaucracy, rapid reaction time, and sense of community to act quickly to counteract rumors and set the record straight with your employees. Your failure to do so could create serious problems for you, personally, and for your organization.

CHAPTER 5

Problems outside the
Organization

"Sustainability is of central importance in building successful partnerships and win-win relationships are a key to sustainability."

Problems outside the Organization

Warning Signal
No.1
Lack of Awareness and Understanding of How to Acquire Donor Monetary and Nonmonetary Resources in a Changing Environment with Changing Priorities

Smaller not-for-profit organizations have to stay on top of their game. They have to know how to acquire donor monetary and nonmonetary resources in a changing environment with changing priorities. They have to be aware of changes such as the downsizing of large organizations, central offices becoming branch offices, small businesses becoming more prevalent, and cooperative efforts becoming more in favor with donors. Not being aware of changes such as these in the external environments in which they work can be disastrous to smaller not-for-profit organizations. It is imperative that you, as the "Observant Leader" of your smaller not-for-profit organization, make certain that systematic ways of monitoring changes in the status of present and potential donors to your organization are in place. Good systems are not hit or miss. They should provide your organization with consistent and reliable feedback. It is important in smaller non-for-profit organizations that the systems developed to monitor changes in the donor base, both present and potential, be as simple as possible. The systems must be doable for smaller organizations. Unnecessary complexity should be avoided.

Your organization's efforts to acquire resources from donors should be based on the awareness and understanding that you gain from your research on their changing situations and priorities.

As you focus on the donor funding priorities that you have discovered, there are some actions that the author of this book recommends that you take in your quest for donor resources.

Actions to Take in Your Quest for Donor Resources:

- Communicate what your organization stands for, what its mission is, and the importance of the mission.
- Communicate your plans for both the immediate and long-term future.
- Communicate the results you have already achieved.
- Demonstrate how your organization is unique; how it is different and better.
- Show donors how they can best achieve their goals and objectives by contributing to your organization.
- Get donors and potential donors involved in the work of your organization.
- Go after the brain power and ideas of donors and potential donors.
- Make efforts to partner with donors and potential donors.
- Hold brainstorming sessions with your Board and employees about how your organization can more effectively expand its active donor base.
- Encourage your Board members and employees to take an active role in communicating to the communities you serve about your organization and its work.
- Involve the recipients of your organization's services in communicating about what these services have meant to them.

As the "Observant Leader" you need to determine which of these actions are most appropriate for your organization. Inherent in this list of actions to assist your organization in acquiring resources are the following assumptions.

Assumptions Inherent in Acquiring Resources from Donors:

- Your organization has to be visible to donors.
- Your mission has to be distinctive and compelling.
- You have to show donors how they can achieve their goals by contributing to the work of your organization.
- You have to make a strong effort to get present and potential donors to participate in some way in the work of your organization. Participation increases commitment.
- You have to communicate what your organization has already accomplished. You have to emphasize the impact you have had on the lives of people. You have to tell stories about these successes.
- You have to make every effort to secure the brain power, ideas, creativity, and other human skills and competencies of present and potential donors. Don't just go after their money.
- Your Board and employees should be involved in your organization's efforts to acquire donor resources.
- You should make every effort to involve the people who benefit from your services in your communications with donors.

The "Observant Leader" knows that it is essential that his or her organization be aware of and understand the changing priorities of donors. The "Observant Leader" also knows that the smaller not-for-profit organization which he leads must be highly visible to present and potential donors. Its unique ability to meet donor needs in ways that are different and better must be clearly evident. Donors must be brought to recognize that they can achieve results in reaching their goals, which they could not achieve on their own, by joining with your organization which has similar goals and objectives. It is essential that there be a win-win relationship between your organization and that of the donor if the relationship is to flourish.

An important strategy that smaller not-for-profit organizations can use in creating a solid relationship with potential donors is to involve them as volunteers in the work of their organizations. Participation as a volunteer provides the opportunity for members of the donor's staff to gain real insights into the work and the impact of this work on the lives of the people being served. This involvement and understanding frequently results in a desire to support the organization's mission.

With regard to the impact of participation on the behavior of people it is usually the case that at performances that encourage audience participation, the applause is almost always the loudest when the audience participates in the program. This is an important fact for the "Observant Leader" to remember in providing leadership for his or her organization.

Participation can be a powerful motivator when worthwhile causes are being pursued. It is an extremely effective way to increase donor commitment to the work of your organization.

The author of this book has had extensive experience in leading advisory committees. A principle which he has learned from these experiences is that it is of critical importance that the members of advisory committees participate actively in the discussions that take place at these meetings if they are to remain committed to the work of the committee. The fact that they are actively participating in the work of the committee gives the members a sense of purpose and accomplishment. If they fail to participate, there is the danger that they will feel that they are wasting their time. This feeling frequently results in poor attendance and finally in dropping out of the committee. This is another example of the power of participation in strengthening and sustaining commitment to the task at hand.

The "Observant Leader" knows that awareness and a real understanding of the priorities of donors serves as the foundation for the involvement of these donors in helping smaller not-for-profit organizations move forward in achieving their mission oriented goals and objectives. This awareness and understanding enables the not-for-profit organization to connect its goals and those of donors in ways that are best tailored to the interests and ability of the donors to participate and are of the greatest value to the not-for-profit organization.

Warning Signal
No. 2
Lack of Awareness of Programs and Services Being Planned and Developed in Your Organization's Fields of Expertise by Other Not-For-Profit Organizations to Serve the Communities You are Presently Serving

It is extremely important that you, as the "Observant Leader," of a smaller not-for-profit organization, be aware of programs and services being planned and developed in your organization's fields of expertise by other not-for-profit organizations to serve the communities you are presently serving.

This is important because not-for-profit organizations should be working in a cooperative manner to meet the large number of pressing needs which must be met in order to improve the quality of life in the communities they are serving. Not-for-profit organizations should only be competing with each other in their efforts to achieve the highest level of service. The goal of each not-for-profit organization should be to become the best it can be in ways that are unique to itself and in which it excels. It needs to know what it is good at and continue to build on its strengths.

Almost all smaller not-for-profit organizations are focused on providing services to certain target groups. In order to have a real impact on its target groups they have to develop areas of expertise that connect with the special needs of these groups. Not-for-profit organizations should not be trying to put each other out of business by attempting to duplicate services but rather should be working together as unique contributing organizations, each with their own service niches, to have a real impact in achieving common goals.

When the "Observant Leader" becomes aware of other not-for-profit organizations developing new programs targeted for the service area being served by the "Observant Leader's" organization, it is important that he or she initiate a dialogue with the parties involved to explore ways in which these organizations can create win-win situations for all the organizations involved and most importantly for the clients being served. As mentioned previously, the need for services to improve the quality of life of the people being served is almost always greater than the capacity of not-for-profit organizations to meet these needs.

Working together is essential if the limited resources of smaller not-for-profit organizations are to be utilized to their fullest extent. Time and energy should not be wasted duplicating services already being provided. It is the author's belief that the greatest results can be achieved if each organization involved retains its unique identity doing what it does best while interacting with other organizations who retain their uniqueness while doing what they do best.

The "Observant Leader" knows what is happening in his or her service areas and works diligently to energize the not-for-profit organizations who are involved to work in a cooperative not competitive manner to achieve the best results for the people being served.

Ideas About Working with Other Not-For-Profit Organizations:

- Frequently the needs are greater than the resources of the not-for-profit organizations attempting to meet the needs.
- Duplication is not a good thing unless the need for the duplication is warranted.
- Most smaller not-for-profit organizations specialize in meeting needs in particular niches which utilize their competencies.
- Smaller not-for-profits need to be differentiated; they should want to be the best at what they do in unique and different ways.
- They should want to complement each other and work together to increase the impact of their work in achieving a common goal.
- They need to know what other organizations in their field are doing and communicate with these organizations on a regular basis.
- If possible it might be desirable to do some joint planning.
- The organizations involved need to have a good "feeling" among their members and a strong commitment to achieving their mission. There should be no hidden agendas.

Warning Signal
No. 3
Your Organization and Private Sector Organizations are Not Benefiting Each Other

It is a warning signal to you, as the "Observant Leader," of a smaller not-for-profit organization, if your organization does not have mutually beneficial relationships with private-for-profit organizations. Private sector organizations have a great deal of vitality, energy, brain power, and expertise that can be of real value to smaller not-for-profit organizations. In return, smaller not-for-profits can be of great value in helping private sector organizations meet their social responsibility obligations to the broader society in which they operate.

A case in point which the author of this book personally observed was a partnership between a local bank and the local headquarters of the Salvation Army. The Salvation Army wanted to operate a "Christmas Castle" in their community whose main purpose was to distribute donated toys to children in the community. The Salvation Army required space to provide this important service to children and the bank provided this space. Employees of the bank and staff and volunteers of the Salvation Army participated actively in this project. This was a win-win-win situation as bank employees, Salvation Army staff and volunteers, and the children benefited from this cooperative effort.

In the experience of the author of this book there have been many occasions in which the private sector has "stepped up to the plate" to work with smaller not-for-profit organizations to help these organizations realize their goals and objectives. Many private sector organizations and their employees gain a great deal of satisfaction from participating with smaller not-for-profit organizations in their efforts to successfully pursue important human improvement initiatives.

In addition to partnerships between smaller not-for-profit organizations and private sector organizations, partnerships can take place between these sectors through private sector individuals volunteering to participate in the work of not-for-profit organizations. Not-for-profit service organizations such as Rotary, Kiwanis, Lions, Soropitimists, and others are often comprised largely of private sector employees who participate as volunteers in the work of their local service organization. These are wonderful examples of private sector employees participating within the framework of a not-for-profit organization to achieve outstanding results.

It is important to remember that win-win relationships are of the essence in any kind of a partnership. Work hard, as the "Observant Leader," to avoid win-lose or lose-lose relationships as your smaller not-for-profit organization works with other organizations in cooperative efforts.

Sustainability is of central importance in building successful partnerships and win-win relationships are a key to sustainability.

Important Points for the "Observant Leader" to Keep in Mind When Working with Private Sector Organizations:

- Respect and learn from the brain power, expertise, and entrepreneurial mindset of this sector.

- Determine mutual interests.

- Help private sector organizations meet their social responsibilities.

- Share your expertise about the importance and power of non-monetary motivators.

- Move beyond stereotyped thinking about the private sector.

- Appreciate the fact that private sector organizations have to make a profit.

- Make every effort to get the private sector organizations involved to participate in some way in the work of your organization.

- Recognize the private sector organizations for their contributions.

As the "Observant Leader," if you find that your organization is doing little or nothing in relating to the private sector, this is an important warning signal that you and your organization should carefully examine the possibilities and opportunities for working together in ways that will enhance the effectiveness, impact, and sustainability of your organization's efforts to move ahead in achieving its mission. These mutual efforts should also be helpful and of value to the private sector organizations participating in these cooperative efforts.

Warning Signal
No. 4
Lack of Productive Relationships with Public Sector Organizations and Elected Officials

The "Observant Leader" of a smaller not-for-profit organization needs to be aware of the importance of his or her organization's relationship with public sector organizations and elected officials. An essential step in building these relationships is for the "Observant Leader" to examine his perceptions of the public sector, its employees, and the elected officials connected with this sector. A major reason for doing this is to attempt to eliminate perceptions which are based on stereotyped thinking. If the "Observant Leader" believes that all the employees in the public sector are inefficient and incompetent he will have to come to understand that this is an erroneous perception and that there are, in fact, many employees in the public sector who are extremely competent and quite efficient, if he is to trust and work cooperatively with them. If he perceives all public officials as "crooks," he will have to change this perception if he is to work cooperatively and productively with them. As in other relationships discussed in this book, there must be a win-win relationship in partnerships between not-for-profit organizations and public sector organizations.

When considering partnerships between not-for-profit organizations and public sector organizations it is important to ask what each of these organizations; not-for-profit and public sector can add to their partnership. Given the emphasis in this book on smaller not-for-profit organizations one must ask the question as to what a smaller not-for-profit organization can add to a partnership with a public sector organization. How can it expand the knowledge base and the skills and competencies of the partnership? In addition, how can it contribute to the performance and positive impact of the work being done by elected officials? One must also ask what contributions the public sector organization can add to the partnership that will achieve results having a greater impact and sustainability. In addition, how can the work of elected officials contribute to the work of smaller not-for-profit organizations?

Following is a listing of some ways in which the author of this book believes that smaller not-for-profit organizations and public sector organizations can contribute to and strengthen the efforts of their partner in the collaborative process. This listing also includes ways in which smaller not-for-profit organizations and elected officials can benefit each other as they work together.

Working Together...Key Contributions

What can smaller not-for-profit organizations contribute to public sector organizations and elected officials?:

- Experience in working with specific target groups.
- Greater flexibility because they are frequently less bureaucratic.
- Greater flexibility because they are frequently more independent.
- Knowledge about non-monetary motivators.
- Knowledge about and experience with community building.
- Enhancement of the reputation of the public sector organization.
- Expansion of the reach of the public sector organization.
- Expertise that improves the quality and effectiveness of legislation that is being prepared.
- Recognition of the good work of the elected officials.
- Recognition of the good work of public sector employees.

What can public sector organizations and elected officials contribute to smaller not-for-profit organizations?:

- Financial support for starting and helping to operate these organizations.
- Financial assistance for physical facilities.
- Educating their constituents about the work of smaller not-for-profit organizations.
- Passing legislation that supports the work of the not-for-profit sector.
- Access to governmental research studies relating to not-for-profit organizations' areas of specialization.
- Access to local, state, national, and international information banks compiled by governmental organizations that enable smaller not-for-profit organizations to look at the bigger picture.
- Support and goodwill from public sector employees in a variety of situations and settings.
- Being an ally in helping to improve the quality of life of the people being served.
- Financial support and training assistance in the acquisition and implementation of technology.

Important Considerations for the "Observant Leader" In working with the public sector and elected officials Keep in mind:

- Not-for-profit organizations and public sector organizations have many common interests. The not-for-profit sector and the public sector are both engaged in efforts to improve the quality of life of their constituents.

- Elected officials will appreciate recognition of the positive work they do and the results they accomplish. It is important to remember that in order to keep their jobs they need to get re-elected.

- Public sector employees are frequently underappreciated. They will usually be most appreciative of recognition you and your organization give them for the good work they accomplish.

- The public sector interfaces with not-for-profit organizations in a variety of ways. There are numerous opportunities for building win-win relationships.

Warning Signal
No. 5
Poor Relationship with the Communications Media

Many people do not understand what a not-for-profit organization is and how it is different from a private sector or public sector organization. In addition, since not-for-profit organizations deal with services which are largely intangible rather than products which are largely tangible, the work a specific not-for-profit organization does may be unclear to the general public. Some smaller not-for-profit organizations may in fact be practically invisible. It is therefore of critical importance to smaller not-for-profits that they develop a close positive working relationship with the various communications media in order to communicate about what they are doing. It is a warning signal to the "Observant Leader" if signs of friction begin to become apparent between his or her not-for-profit organization and the communications media. Such developing friction requires immediate attention and action.

The author of this book, based on his observations as a practitioner in the field, suggests several steps that the "Observant Leader" can take to maintain an excellent relationship with the communications media.

Key Steps in Maintaining Excellent Relationships with the Communications Media:

- Focus on developing win-win relationships with the media.
- Involve the media in sponsorships that support the quality of life in the community.
- Involve the media in joint undertakings with the public, private, and nonprofit sector.
- Supply the media with stories and other information with a human interest focus and emphasis.
- Include members of the media on your Board of Directors and appropriate advisory committees.
- Be careful about competing with the communications media regarding advertising revenue.
- Stress the fact that your organization is a private organization governed by a Board of Directors of unpaid volunteers.
- Publicize and emphasize the work that the communications media does to contribute to the success of your organization in achieving its mission.

Using these suggestions as guidelines in your organization's relationship with the communications media should prove to be of real value as you work with them to successfully inform the communities you serve about your organization and why it is deserving of their support.

Warning Signal
No. 6
Difficult Influential Individuals in Your Service Areas Who are Unhappy with You and Your Organization

A warning signal to the "Observant Leader" is the presence of difficult influential individuals in your service area who are unhappy with you and your organization. These individuals may, in many cases, be quite emotional about the specific issues which make them unhappy. It is important that the "Observant Leader" act to resolve these situations as quickly as possible.

Following are some suggestions that the author of this book has found to be useful in his experiences in the field. These suggestions are: determine specifically what is bothering the individual, identify in detail what the individual's interests are regarding the resolution of the issues in question, determine areas of mutual interest, and develop and agree on a win-win solution. This process may be implemented through a one on one meeting with the individual or through a meeting involving several individuals. If a one on one meeting is not successful it may prove to be useful to involve another individual who is a friend of the unhappy person or a person who is respected for some other reasons by the unhappy party. It may also be useful to invite the unhappy individual to meet with a representative group such as your executive committee or Board of Directors to discuss the issue in question if this appears to be a productive way of resolving the situation. Identifying mutual interests is of great importance in this process. So too is the desirability of decreasing the level of emotion in the interactions with the difficult influential person. If there is to be a thoughtful rational dialogue between the parties involved, emotional outbursts need to be kept to a minimum in order to achieve an openness to the ideas being discussed. There is a need for the kind of listening that is necessary for a real understanding of the issues at hand. The "Observant Leader" needs to be straightforward, honest, and open about why he or she and the organization are pursuing a particular course of action. There must also be an openness to the ideas being expressed by the disagreeing individual.

In many cases an individual who is a major antagonist of the organization will become one of its major advocates as a result of really understanding the reasons for the actions being taken as they relate to the overall mission. Turning difficult antagonistic influential people into enthusiastic supporters of the organization requires leaders to focus both on the needs of the individual and the needs of the organization. This effort requires patience, insight, and good communication skills. As mentioned previously, smaller not-for-profit organizations need all the friends they can get. They have to have as few antagonists as possible who require an inordinate amount of their time and energy and diminish their ability to lead their organizations in the successful achievement of their missions. The "Observant Leader" pays careful attention to difficult influential individuals and works to convert them to enthusiastic supporters of his or her organization.

CHAPTER 6

Wisdom from the "Observant Leader"

"In your role as the 'Observant Leader' it is important for you to realize that your role has unique responsibilities and that other people have certain expectations and perceptions of you because you are a leader."

Wisdom from the "Observant Leader"

This chapter serves as a way to re-emphasize some key points presented in this book as well as to introduce some new materials that the author believes to be of significant importance to the leadership practitioner in smaller not-for-profit organizations.

The ideas presented in this chapter deal with leadership mindset and behavior, Board behavior, focusing on and sustaining the mission, financial well-being, and awareness of and communication with the internal and external environments of the organization.

There is also a list of warning signals concerning the identification of "back stabbers"; people you want to watch out for as you go about your work in the leadership role. In addition, there is a listing of things the author believes you should pay particular attention to if you are interested in keeping your job.

In your role as the "Observant Leader" it is important for you to realize that your role has unique responsibilities and that other people have certain expectations and perceptions of you because you are a leader. Some of these unique characteristics of the leadership role are also highlighted in this chapter. As you think about a particular idea presented in Chapter 6 you may want to re-read the section of the book relating to it in order to put it into the proper context.

Factors that Differentiate a Leader from Other Members of the Organization:

- You have to have a clear vision of where you want your organization to go and lead the way to make this vision a reality.
- You report to a Board.
- You are responsible for the operational side of the enterprise.
- People view you in a different way. In many cases they view you as "the organization."
- You are of critical importance in creating the "character" and the style of the organization.
- You have to project an air of confidence and competence in what you are doing which resonates with the overall organization.
- You are held accountable for the performance of your organization.

The Leadership Benefits of Self-Confidence and High Self-Esteem:

- A willingness to see and pursue a range of possibilities.
- A willingness to test limits.
- A belief that you are capable of facing the challenges of leadership.
- Being adventuresome in spirit and outlook.
- Being able to act with courage in the face of fear.
- Having the courage to make difficult decisions.
- Having the courage to lead by example.
- Having the courage to be proactive.
- Being able to inspire confidence in others by projecting a confident image.
- Believing that you are a worthy human being and that others are also worthy and deserving of respect.

How Do You as the "Observant Leader" Keep the Board, Management, and Employees Strongly Committed to the Vision and Mission of the Organization?

- Be as clear as possible about the vision and purpose of your organization.
- Have clear short term goals and report regularly on progress in reaching these goals.
- Keep the mission statement in front of the people on a regular basis.
- Relate regularly to clients of the organization and get feedback from them concerning how your organization is improving the quality of their lives.
- Work hard to transform individual commitment and motivation into organizational commitment and motivation regarding the mission.
- Transform self-interest into organizational-interest.
- Recognize successes in achieving the mission in important and creative ways on a regular basis.
- Point out regularly how what your organization is doing is different and better than other's efforts.
- Bring in other people who can further energize work on your mission and bring more excitement and power to it.
- Engender pride in the work done and outcomes achieved with regard to your mission.
- Share what you are doing with others who are interested in achieving the same outcomes.
- Keep your mission statement "fresh" by keeping the core and changing the peripheral factors to be in keeping with the times.

How Does the Leader Find out What is Really Going on?

- Get out and talk to a range of people.
- Have consistent and accurate systems of feedback.
- Don't just talk to your friends, talk as well to people who don't like what you are doing.
- Spend time talking to the recipients of your services.
- Do a variety of jobs yourself in order to increase your insight.
- Study the behavior of other organizations in your fields of service.
- Arrange for times when you are visible and approachable.
- Have an active schedule of small group meetings which are free wheeling in nature.
- Encourage and reward suggestions for improving all aspects of your operations.
- Focus on getting input on the most important aspects of your organization- the things that really make a difference.

What Do You, as the Leader, Need to Know About the Culture of Your Organization?

- What are its values, beliefs, norms, and assumptions?
- Who are the leaders of your informal organization (the organization that does not appear on the formal organization chart)?
- What are the major sub groups within the informal organization?
- What are the relationships between the members of the leadership team in the formal organization?
- Who are the key players in the grapevine (the communication network of the informal organization)?
- What is the real power structure in the formal organization?
- Who are the decision-makers in the informal organization?
- Who are the most respected individuals in the informal organization?
- Who are the most respected individuals in the formal organization?
- What is the level of trust in your organization?
- What is the level of morale in your organization?
- What is the tone (the "feeling" level) of your organization?

- What is the level of commitment to the mission of your organization?
- What are the growth characteristics of your organization?
- What are the agendas of the leaders of the informal organization?
- What are the important cliques in your organization and what are their agendas?
- What are the major changes taking place in your organization?
- Who are the most productive employees?

Leader Mindset and Behavior Impeding Communication Feedback:

- Not getting out into the organization.
- Not talking with diverse individuals and groups.
- Not having meetings which include all the members of your organization.
- Not wanting to hear bad news.
- Lack of rewards for feedback.
- Failure to take action after receiving feedback.
- Not paying attention to changes in the external landscape.
- Attitude that you have all the answers.
- Belief that you understand what has been communicated based on presumptions.
- Failure to use appropriate technology.
- Not realizing the importance of feedback-the feeling that no news is good news.
- Getting feedback only from your friends.
- Being influenced by "they say."
- The fact that you don't hear complaints.
- A failure to be proactive.
- Not being tuned into the grapevine and its key communicators.
- Receiving only good news.
- Not paying attention to and understanding cultural differences.
- Focusing on what is wrong with ideas rather than listening to them.
- Having fears that impede communication.

Importance of Participation in Achieving Mission Centered Goals:

- Participation increases commitment.
- Participation in sub groups and in the entire group encourages teamwork.
- Participation encourages a sense of personal worth.
- Participation supports commitment to the overall mission.
- Participation supports continuity of effort.
- Participation encourages the desire for performance feedback.
- Participation encourages continuing action rather than being passive.
- Participation is personally motivating.

The "Observant Leader" Wishlist Concerning the Chairman of the Board:

You want a Chairman who:

- Is respected by the Board.
- You respect.
- You can trust and will stand by you.
- Is emotionally and intellectually compatible with you.
- Is a team player, values input from others and is a good listener.
- Can be decisive and does what he says he will do.
- Is willing to take calculated risks.
- Understands his roles and responsibilities.
- Has a good sense of humor.
- Cares about the well-being of others.
- You want to have a role in the selection of the Chairman.
- You want some continuity in the position of Chairman.

Reasons Why the Board Should Want the "Observant Leader" to Have Appropriate Input into the Selection Process of the Board Chair and Members of the Board:

- The Board should want to have a Board Chair and members who are compatible with the leader.

- The Board should want to have input from the "Observant Leader" concerning the competencies the leader believes are important at this point in time in new Board members and a new Board Chair.

- The Board should want to have the leader meet potential Board members and get his or her reaction to them before they are officially brought on board.

- The Board should want to have the leader brief potential Board members about the state of the organization and its future plans as part of the selection process and as the first step in an ongoing orientation process.

- The Board should want the participation of the leader in the Board selection and orientation process to serve as a model concerning the way in which the Board and the "Observant Leader" work together in a win-win relationship in running the organization.

Warning Signals Concerning Financial Well-Being:

- Inadequate financial reserves.
- Board members who don't appreciate the importance of financial reserves.
- A Chief Financial Officer you can't trust.
- A Chief Financial Officer who is incompetent.
- Board members who embark on expensive ego-centered ventures.
- Inadequate procedures for dealing with layoffs.
- Declining membership.
- Changes in the priorities of donors.
- Businesses which are becoming regional rather than local.
- Increasing overhead.
- A tendency to make facilities and furnishings more luxurious.
- New initiatives by organizations in your areas of service that may erode your client base.
- Poorly thought through fundraising efforts.
- Board members who think you are a charitable organization for other organizations.
- You, as a leader, are not in control of your organization's finances.
- Projects that have little or nothing to do with your mission.
- Inability to convince your constituents that the services that you are providing are worthy of their support.

The "Observant Leader" needs to understand what impact its financial condition may have on the overall organization.

The mission is of the first importance however ...

If Finances aren't in Good Order the Following Could Happen:

- You could lose your job.
- The morale of the organization may suffer.
- The level of anxiety may rise.
- People could have trouble focusing on their jobs.
- People may have trouble focusing on the mission.
- Organizational conflict may increase.
- The level of trust could decrease.
- Risk taking may decrease.
- Innovation may decrease.
- Organizational energy may decrease.

The "Observant Leader" needs to pay continuing attention to the financial condition of the organization.

Reasons for the Financial Vulnerability of Smaller Not-For-Profits:

- Lack economy of scale.
- Significant dependence on volunteers.
- Limited donor base because of limited service area.
- Unpredictability of funding sources.
- May be partially dependent on support from the private sector.
- May be partially dependent on support from the public sector.
- Unable to afford essential managerial competencies.
- Having to operate out of deficient facilities which impair the ability to generate income.
- Unpredictable overhead expenses.
- Can be highly susceptible to changes in the economy.
- Because they frequently deal with services (intangibles) rather than concrete products they may have trouble communicating to potential donors how the money and other resources they receive are being transformed into concrete results.
- Frequently dependent on fundraisers to fill in the financial gaps.
- Lack adequate financial reserves.
- Ego oriented expensive projects of Board members.

- Poor decisions on even small matters cannot be dealt with financially because of small margin for error.
- They are unable to project a clear, motivating, exciting, important image of their mission to their various potential constituencies.

Some Advantages of Utilizing Volunteers in Your Smaller Not-For-Profit Organization:

- Being able to increase the size of your workforce when you can't afford to hire additional paid employees.
- Acquiring competencies that you would not otherwise be able to acquire.
- Securing role models of commitment that will inspire your paid workforce.
- Acquiring representatives of your organization who will communicate what you are doing to the communities that you relate to in which they are members.
- Having individuals in your organization from communities that you relate to who can provide you with feedback about how these communities perceive your organization and what it is doing.
- Having individuals on board in your organization who can teach you about the importance of non-monetary motivators in energizing your workforce.
- Being able to receive honest and accurate feedback from individuals who are not afraid to speak openly because they are not being paid monetarily by your organization.

What are Some Characteristics of Potential Back Stabbers?:

- Individuals who are overwhelmingly ambitious.
- Individuals who are very manipulative in nature.
- Individuals who agree with almost everything you say or do.
- Individuals who go out of their way to ingratiate themselves to you.
- Individuals who spend a lot of time criticizing other people.
- Individuals who tell untruths about other people.
- Individuals who are self-important with big egos.
- Individuals who attempt to be perceived as your mentor.
- Individuals who have little respect for the inherent worth of other people.

How to Keep Your Job:

- Keep your financial situation in good order.
- Develop a close ongoing relationship with the Board Chair.
- Build positive relationships with the leaders in the communities you serve.
- Be proactive in dealing with changes in the internal and external environments.
- Get feedback on a continuing basis from a diverse group of people.
- Get continuing feedback from the clients of your organization.
- Pay close attention to the "tone" of your organization.
- Pay close attention to funding sources.
- Keep communicating how your organization is different and better.
- Report regularly on the successes your organization is having.
- Build a personal network of support.
- Be involved in the hiring process.
- Be involved in the Board and Board Chair selection process.
- Don't make promises you can't keep.

Conclusion

Not-for-profit organizations are an important and distinctive feature of American society. A majority of these institutions are smaller in size. They are of great importance in transmitting the values, beliefs, norms, and assumptions of our culture.

Leading these smaller not-for-profit organizations is a challenging and difficult job. They require superior leadership in order to survive and prosper.

The leaders of these organizations frequently have limited resources at their command and have little room in their decision making for errors. They have to be right most of the time.

The author of this book is concerned about the turnover rate of the leaders of these smaller not-for-profit organizations. He believes that in order to have a real impact on the organizations they lead that leaders have to be around for an adequate period of time. What is an adequate period of time to have a positive impact on the well-being and contributions of a smaller not-for-profit organization will, of course, vary from situation to situation.

This book identifies warning signals that can alert leaders of smaller not-for-profit organizations concerning present and potential problems that could undermine their personal well-being and the well-being of the organizations they lead. It is the hope of the author that an awareness of these warning signals will enable the leader to take actions that will result in successful outcomes for both the leader and the organization. Such actions require an "Observant Leader."

Included in this book have been numerous suggestions concerning actions that "Observant Leaders" can take to increase their longevity and inpact on the organizations they lead. These suggestions are based on the author's experiences "in the trenches" as a practitioner in a variety of not-for-profit organizations. The author can relate in a very personal way to the leadership demands of these complex institutions.

Board members play an extremely important role in the success of smaller not-for-profit organizations. It is of the greatest importance that these Board members understand how difficult the job of leaders in these organizations is and how they can best help to encourage and support their efforts. The general public also has a critical role to play in supporting the efforts of these smaller not-for-profit organizations which are involved in a variety of ways in improving the quality of life for so many people in the communities in which they live as well as in the broader society.

It is the author's hope that this book will result in an increase in the number of "Observant Leaders" who will lead not-for-profit organizations with an increased commitment to have a significant personal impact on the work of their organizations. Hopefully the book will help them not only to increase their longevity in their jobs but also increase their contributions to their constituents.

The need for "Observant Leaders" is of the utmost importance if not-for-profit organizations are to have the kind of leadership that is required for them to meet the challenges facing them as they work to improve the quality of life in their communities and the broader society.

The author hopes that you will become an "Observant Leader" as the result of reading this book.

CPSIA information can be obtained
at www.ICGtesting.com
Printed in the USA
BVHW041954160821
614558BV00020B/340

9 781937 721756